Clearing Cardigan

Lieutenant General James Thomas Brudenell, 7th Earl of Cardigan at the Charge of the Light Brigade 1854

Stephen Bloom

CONTENTS

PREFACE

Generally speaking I should really know of this tragic military event from some distant history lessons about Cardigan and the Charge of the Light Brigade way back in 1854. I also remember a terrible old film in black and white with a dashing Errol Flynn in it, plus a more modern and excellent 1968 version with Cardigan portrayed by Trevor Howard. *"Forward, the Light Brigade! Was there a man dismay'd? Not tho' the soldier knew, someone had blunder'd: theirs not to make reply, theirs not to reason why, theirs but to do and die: into the valley of death rode the six hundred."* – Alfred, Lord Tennyson December 9th 1854. Into the valley of death rode the 600, said the poet laureate. I find that things were actually quite different. For a start it should have been the 700 (673 men by most accounts). The Light Brigade was destroyed? In all about 113 men were killed – or nearly 17% of the force, but even more were wounded – 134 men, or nearly 20% of the brigade. That's 37%, or more than a third of the men killed and wounded. Over 70.5% (about 475) horses were also killed.

Did the brigade attack their Russian enemy at the end of the correct valley, or did Lord Cardigan or Lord Lucan select the wrong one, and why? Cardigan blamed his brother-in-law Lucan for the error. Lucan blamed Raglan, the commander-in-chief for his ambiguous attack order. And what had Captain Nolan to do with it; carrying the message from Raglan to Lucan and then perhaps pointing down the wrong valley – before he could correct the error to Cardigan, Nolan was blown to bits on the battlefield, the first casualty of the charge. Unlike General George Custer's battlefield in Montana, the valley of death has not been preserved to the same extent. Farmer's fields cover the area with what looks like vineyards in places. Where the Russian guns and cavalry stood in astonishment at the far end of the valley near a Roman style aqueduct now stands Ukrainian houses (also half way down the valley, too).

The hilly redoubts on the south side of the valley called the Causeway Heights by the British, once held allied cannon manned by Turks until they were seized by Russians in a prelude to Cardigan's charge, are now well eroded with time. But much of it still remains, and with aerial photographs and ancient maps I hope to show the close location of where battle was fought. To the end of his days and much since then, the 7th Earl of Cardigan, James Thomas Brudenell, was often blamed for the disaster. He was a strict man with his men and no wonder, since as colonel of his regiment (11th Hussars) he had to pay and maintain it mostly at his own expense. That was the way of things back then.

In the chapters that follow I shall examine other historian's findings and comments, and particularly the history and newspaper transcripts from 1854. So, the first two volumes of this work are a resume of this war, as I understand it, and the reasons it came about. Thereafter in this third volume I shall go through Inkerman, which is necessary to understand the Crimean war, and in the last volume cover any salient points in my effort to credit Cardigan. In the finale, I believe the reader will understand the true facts and must conclude that Cardigan himself was just one of many brave heroes during that bloody day of October 1854; that he certainly was not to blame for what happened to his brigade, and really deserves high recognition to some degree. Included also you will find a vast number of photos of the people involved, where available, and battle scene location maps, which I think give a nice realism to things. After all, as with General Custer back in 1876, it is nice to put a face to a name, isn't it?

Stephen Bloom, England 2017

PHOTOGRAPHS OF PEOPLE INVOLVED

All photos freely available on the world wide net, unless otherwise stated. John Roebuck MP by Maull & Polyblank. Harry Jones by the Marjorie and Leonard Vernon Collection/Fenton.

ILLUSTRATIONS

1. WHAT FOLLOWED NEXT?

Cardigan meets Raglan

When roll muster was complete and Lord Cardigan was aware of the losses inflicted upon his brigade, he rode up to Lord Raglan, who by now with his staff had descended into the north valley, to report. Both men must have been seething with anger at this meeting. In what was described by attendant witnesses as a severe and angry exchange, Raglan, shaking with rage more than his staff had ever seen before, said 'what did you mean, sir, by attacking a battery in front, contrary to all the usages of warfare and the customs of the service?'

Cardigan's indignant reply was 'my Lord, I hope you will not blame me, for I received the order to attack from my superior officer in front of the troops.' He then proceeded to relate the part he had taken in the battle. The narrative convinced Raglan of the correctness of Cardigan's actions. In correspondence, a few days later, Raglan described Cardigan as having acted with great steadiness, gallantry and perseverance.

Lucan meets Raglan

A short time later, Lord Raglan came upon Lord Lucan and said to him 'you have lost the Light Brigade!' Lucan's reply was to deny he had lost the brigade, and that he was only carrying out the orders, written and verbal, conveyed to him by Captain Nolan. Surprisingly, Lord Raglan did not have a copy on his person of either the third or fourth orders issued that day. Lord Lucan held the original order, written by Richard Airey. Instead of querying it at this stage, Raglan replied, according to the divisional commander, 'Lord Lucan, you were a lieutenant general and should therefore have exercised your discretion and not approving of the charge, should not have caused it to be made.'

Lucan could counter this easily, because Raglan, from his location on the Sapoune Heights, had a much better view of the valley below than those actually below in it; to disobey such an order from the commander-in-chief, who had superior knowledge of the situation, was not possible. Not even Cardigan, Lucan nor Captain Nolan could see the attempt at removing British guns on the Causeway Heights by the Russians; only those up on Sapoune Heights could see what was going on, if indeed the Russians were trying to remove them.

Raglan's thoughts

It was necessary, of course, for the allied commander-in-chief to write with haste home, to announce what had happened before those gentlemen of the press distributed their story. Here Raglan confessed that the charge of the Light Brigade was a heavy misfortune, the loss of which he felt most deeply [1]. Privately, he thought the charge was perhaps the finest thing ever attempted, despite French General Bosquet saying at the time 'it is splendid but it is not war!'

Russians reinforce

Once the dust had settled on the battlefield, General Liprandi decided to reinforce the Causeway Heights with Odessa Regiment and others, until there were eight battalions plus artillery as far as Redoubt 3. This action was seen clearly by Colin Campbell and his 93rd Highlanders, and prompted him to ride to the Duke of Cambridge (1st Infantry Division) and suggested the duke dissuade Sir Cathcart (4th Infantry Division) from attacking further that Russian held redoubt. The duke declined to interfere, and so Sir Colin rode off to find Sir Cathcart in person. As we have seen, Cathcart had stopped advancing at Redoubt 4 anyway, and so no further advance was made by his division.

The aftermath of the charge of the Light Brigade – Russia still held redoubts 1 – 3 (courtesy Google earth).

Raglan's next move

The position of Balaclava was still precarious, with the Russian's in control of the Causeway Heights and reinforcing Redoubts 1-3, but there was still a lack of available troops to carry on the siege of Sevastopol and protect the British base at Balaclava at the same time. French Commander Francois Canrobert was still convinced that Liprandi's advance as far as Redoubt 3 was just a ploy to bring allied troops into the Balaclava valley, and enable the Russian's to attack elsewhere and lift the siege of Sevastopol. Two British divisions were already on the plain: 1st Infantry (Cambridge) and 4th Infantry (Cathcart), but these were needed long term to work in the siege lines.

The decimated Heavy Brigade, the pitiful remains of the Light Brigade, Colin Campbell's 93rd Regiment and the French Chasseurs d'Afrique were the only forces immediately available. Lord Raglan must have dreaded trying to convince his French counterpart that action was necessary to protect the British port. A victory, however small, for the Russians would present a moral boosting victory for those trapped inside Sevastopol. Incredibly, it was decided, in the light of French sensitivities, to leave the Russians in control of Redoubts 1 – 3 and reinforce the remaining three! Accordingly, Sir George Cathcart manned Redoubt 4 with artillery and Turkish troops, and a fusillade (discharge from a number of firearms fired simultaneously) put silence to Russian guns nearby.

This long range attack ended at 4 p.m. when the Russians were left in control of their conquests; thus the battle of Balaclava came to an end. But at what cost? The allies lost 600 officers and men killed and wounded that day, with about 15 uninjured men taken into captivity. The Light Brigade alone lost 262. The Russians lost 627 men killed or wounded, according to the official return endorsed by General Todleben.

But was Balaclava a victory, and if so, for whom? The allies or the Russians? The answer here is fairly straight forward – the victory was for the allies, because the Russians failed to capture Balaclava. They also lost more men killed and wounded. But then in truth it was really a stalemate. What a price to pay for the allies, and the Light Brigade in particular, for poor generalship.

Lucky escapes

The survivors surely discussed the fates of their missing comrades and their own lucky escapes after roll call had been made. Up on the Sapoune Heights, during the charge into the gates of hell, Mrs Fanny Duberly, wife of Henry the paymaster of the 8th Hussars and at that time, accompanying Raglan, exclaimed 'what can those skirmishers be doing?' Followed by 'good god! It is the Light Brigade!' Many men on the field found Cossacks riding about, intent on looting saddles from dead horses. In fact, the Russians held a market later in the day to sell them on; also, sabres and helmets recovered from the battlefield. Many injured, retreating members of the Light Brigade reported that they only had to point a gun at Cossacks for them to run away [2].

Men carried their saddles from their dead horses back to the British lines; amongst them, Cornet Denzil Chamberlayne. Cossacks were seen stabbing the dead and wounded with their lances, provoking many apparently dead corpses to suddenly get to their feet and run for it – amongst them, Cornet George Clowes from 8th Hussars, despite bleeding badly from his wounds. Others who could not move died bravely, or fought to the end with their hand guns; believed amongst them was Captain Thomas Goad of the 13th, last seen wounded, sitting on the ground, gun in hand.

Three main groups from the Light Brigade had earlier made their escape; those led by Shewell, Paget and a third under Corporal Morley of 17th Lancers. He had veered left on to the lower slopes of the Causeway Heights, where a square of Russian infantry fired from almost point blank range and reduced further the escapees. One of the men, Private James Wightman, had received many injuries during the chase: struck on the forehead and through the shoulder by Russian bullets, he only just managed to pull himself free from his dead horse when he was further cut in the neck and stabbed in the back several times by a clumsy Cossack with a lance.

He was also stabbed through the hand and could not draw his sword, but managed to make good his survival by throwing sand in the Cossack's face! He was captured with others by the Russians. Comradeship came to the fore during this dramatic retreat to safety. Captain Augustus Webb was heading back but stopped when he realized he had a severe leg wound and the pain was such that every step by his horse was just too much to bear. Sergeant John Berryman of 17th Lancers saw him halt; Webb could not move because of the pain, so Berryman, with assistance from Sergeant John Farrell and Corporal Malone of 13th Light Dragoons, helped him dismount and carried him up the hill towards safety.

For these acts of bravery in the face of enemy fire, all three rescuing men received the Victoria Cross medal; Corporal Malone, who was keeping the Cossacks at bay alone, was mortally wounded during their retreat. Captain Morris had made his escape, but loss of blood had slowed him down until he collapsed near safety. News of his collapse reached the lines and George Cathcart, being present, gave permission for Captain Ewart, one of Raglan's aides, to investigate.

The captain passed the dead body of Captain Nolan before finding Morris, whom he could not move on his own; a mounted 17th Lancer, Private George Smith, was sent back for a stretcher party. Assistant Surgeon William Cattell of 5th Dragoons and Surgeon James Mouat with Sergeant Charles Wooden, was sent to the rescue. Private George Mansell fended away any approaching Cossacks. Morris was semi-conscious by this time and muttering a prayer to the Lord to have mercy upon his soul, according to Sir John Blunt, Lord Lucan's interpreter. Surgeon Mouat and Sergeant Wooden received the Victoria Cross for their efforts.

Dust settles

When the smoke and dust had cleared following the retreat of the Light Brigade, the battlefield was clearly visible. The dead and wounded from the charge, along with their horses, lay scattered along the route into the gates of hell. As in the later battle of the Little Bighorn in 1876, the wounded cried out for water. Passing comrades did their best to help them limp away to safety. Modern day first aid existed in 1854 too: Privates Mitchell and Pollard found a critically injured man gurgling and laid him upon his side, so that he 'would be better able to relieve himself of the blood than by lying on his back' [3].

Those two cavalry troopers could now see the effects of Russian guns on the brigade during the advance; most visible and upsetting was the devastation brought upon the horses of the regiments. One man called for help because he was trapped beneath his dead horse; together, they managed to extricate him but he was too badly injured to move any further.

'You can do no more for me. Look out for yourselves!' he said to them. Many riderless horses ran about the place wounded or in fear, and to capture one of these meant almost certain salvation.

Private Robert Farquharson of 4th Light Dragoons changed horses several times before finally escaping on a Cossack pony and having to defend himself from a pursuing Cossack, whose face he had slashed open with his sabre. Many a man saw off Cossack riders during that perilous chase.

Burial of Captain Nolan

Controversy surrounding Captain Nolan continued even when the charge was complete. Being the nearest dead officer to British lines, he was first to be buried; apparently on the slopes of the Causeway Heights in a shallow grave where probably he remains to this day - the location was not recorded! Captain Brandling from Royal Horse Artillery arranged this and reported later that Nolan's chest was broken away and the gold lace and cloth from his jacket very much burnt. Close to the location of the grave stood the remains of the Light Brigade, forming up for roll call. Lord Cardigan confirmed that only 195 mounted men capable of fight were listed.

Aftermath of the charge

The injured were left with the surgeons, and those men without horses sent back to camp nearby. Troop Sergeant Major George Smith from 11th Hussars discovered pieces of human flesh on his uniform; these were from Private Young when his arm was blown off! The sergeant was visibly upset by the loss of his horse, and his orderly room clerk made Smith some tea to calm him down. The time of day he described as being about midday. Few men had eaten since the day before; the reason was that they had been on their way to breakfast when the early morning alert had sounded. Now at midday, the brigade farriers went about their grim tasking of shooting injured or dying horses.

How the survivors must have felt that afternoon and evening can only be imagined: elation at taking part in what was clearly a historic military event; sadness at the loss of so many friends and horses, and anger at the failure of any support from the Heavy Brigade. Support would have probably sent the whole Russian army packing, but despite the great hole punched through the centre by the Light Brigade, the opportunity for victory was lost no thanks to the failed support of the Heavy Brigade. With the Russians still in command of the eastern part of the Causeway Heights, orders were sent down for the Light Brigade not to light fires or make much noise that night. Most of the men could not sleep, but rather hung around in groups mulling over events of the day. Corporal James Nunnerley of 17th Lancers slept alone in his tent that he normally shared between nine other men!

Legend is born

William Russell, *Times* correspondent, was composing his next despatch home about the charge on the afternoon following the disaster; he described Lord Raglan as being much moved with anger, and having given it hot to Lord Lucan – to Lord Cardigan he had also given a tremendous wigging. Russell described the Light Brigade as being 607 men in number, which was picked up back home by Lord Tennyson in his immortal poem 'the charge of the Light Brigade.' Thus, he began his famous prose:

'Half a league, half a league, half a league onward, all in the valley of death rode the six hundred. Forward, the Light Brigade! Charge for the guns! he said: Into the valley of death rode the six hundred.'

Of course, the true figure was nearer 700 men, but by that time the poem was in print and alteration could not be made. The truth was quickly becoming muddied by men who were present giving their stories to the British press; some of their tales were coloured, as one would expect since many men were illiterate, and the journalists gave a hand in the stories. One such was Private John Vahey, who was a 'volunteer butcher' from 17th Lancers and had been drunk the night before and on the day of the charge. His story appears in a magazine called '*Soldiering and Scribbling*,' and he appears, in his bloody butcher's clothes, to have purloined a stray Russian pony (after the charge of the Heavy Brigade) upon which he joined 17th Lancers in time for the charge [4].

Much of what Vahey says must be taken with caution. He says, for example, that Lord Cardigan signalled the charge and then Captain Nolan was hit and killed; we know that Cardigan maintained a rapid trot until within 250 yards of the Russian guns, long after Nolan was killed at the onset of the attack. But some of his points are valid as well. He describes on contact with the enemy how swarming Russians would not come to close quarters with the sword, and could not use their pistols because they were too thick. In other words, they might hit their own colleagues at close range.

During the retreat, Vahey stopped to pick up a wounded man before carrying him to safety and the surgeons. Later, Vahey was re-arrested for being drunk the night before and taken, he says, before Lord Lucan, who let him off punishment for his good use of liberty during the charge of the Light Brigade! Sergeant John Pardoe of 1st Royal Dragoons doubts, however, the business of Vahey being brought before Lucan, since Vahey was missing for several days after the charge by the brigade [5]. Vahey's tale was not the only testimony to surface after the event.

2. JOURNALISM AND LITTLE INKERMAN

Journalist and artist

By way of comparison, journalist William Russell of the *Times* had been accompanying the army and reporting to his newspaper the suffering of the British army during the campaign. Because of this, he had been 'snubbed' by a number of senior officers of the British army, but not everyone. On the day of the charge, Russell was up on Sapoune Heights with the senior staff, watching events; later he interviewed many men and officers but did not quote them verbatim in his despatches. Russell's despatch was written about two o'clock in the afternoon following the charge of the Light Brigade, but did not appear in print in newspapers until Tuesday 14th November 1854. That's how long transport took in those days! He describes the charge as an exhibition of brilliant valour, an excess of courage and of such daring against a savage and barbarian enemy! [6]

William Russell

William Simpson

William Filder

Whilst trying to give mainly his own opinions of what he had seen with his own eyes, Russell began stating that some quarters of the army believed the British cavalry had not been properly handled since landing in the Crimea by its leaders, with indecision and excessive caution! He goes on to describe General Airey giving the written order for the cavalry to advance to Captain Nolan, whom he describes in his text as a brave soldier; he incorrectly describes thirty Russian guns as being drawn across the valley floor.

According to William Russell, when Lord Lucan read the message he said to Nolan 'where are we to advance to?' at which Nolan pointed his finger to the line of the Russian guns and replied 'there are the enemy and there are the guns, sir, before them; it is your duty to take them,' or words to that effect! The message was relayed reluctantly to Lord Cardigan. Interestingly, the journalist goes on to describe the normal maxims of war: that cavalry never acts without a support; that infantry should be close at hand when cavalry carry guns, and that it is necessary to have on the flank of a line of cavalry some squadrons in column, the attack on the flank being most dangerous.

These, in my opinion, were as Russell describes the essential 'maxims of war' and should have been satisfied in full before Lord Cardigan was sent on his suicidal mission – this was clearly a serious oversight by Lord Lucan, who did have the resting Heavy Brigade available as a 'support' and the unreliable Sir George Cathcart's 4th Division as infantry to be 'close at hand'; neither were fully alerted to their duty, although the Heavy Brigade did make a token gesture. William Russell goes on next to describe the size of the units facing the enemy when they lined up to advance: 4th Light Dragoons 118 men; 8th Hussars 104 men; 11th Hussars 110 men; 13th Light Dragoons 130 men, and 17th Lancers 145 men – hence a total of 607, which was picked up by Alfred Lord Tennyson in his immortal poem 'the charge of the Light Brigade' as the gallant 600.

As the Russian guns opened fire, the brigade swept proudly on; glittering in the morning sun with all the pride and splendour of war. Those on the Sapoune Hills, along with William Russell, could scarcely believe their eyes as the drama unfolded; surely those men were not going to charge an army in position, Russell asked? The brigade advanced in two lines (three in fact), quickening their pace as they closed the enemy. At 1200 yards, the journalist says, the Russian guns opened fire, but the Light Brigade continued on and flew into the smoke of the batteries, and were then lost from view.

The plain was, however, strewn with their bodies and the carcasses of dead horses. They were exposed to an oblique fire from the batteries on the hills on both sides, as well as direct fire from musketry (the guns on the Fedioukine Hills had, by this time, been silenced by the charge of the French cavalry, so this could not be precisely correct). Through the clouds of smoke the witness and the British high command saw the sabres flashing as the Light Brigade engaged the enemy (the distance from Lord Raglan's location on the Sapoune Heights to the Russian guns was about 3 miles).

By 11:35 the battle was over and by two o'clock in the afternoon roll call was complete, and William Russell included the missing, wounded and dead in his dispatches home. These he gives as follows: 4th Light Dragoons 79 lost; 8th Hussars 66 lost; 11th Hussars 85 lost; 13th Light Dragoons 69 lost and 17th Lancers 110 lost – a total loss of 409, or 67.38% of the total attack force! Hence we have annihilation of the Light Brigade, which was not quite true.

Back in England, this journalist's dispatches were the only means of informing the public and the army left behind in barracks about what had happened in the Crimea; of course, it was mostly taken as the gospel truth. Drawings of the charge of the Light Brigade were inaccurate too, despite artist William Simpson, who arrived in the Crimea in the middle of November 1854, doing his best to acquire accurate information from those who took part, including Lord Cardigan.

Cardigan was desirous that he was seen in any paintings leading the charge, which was duly done, but in most the middle row of the brigade was inaccurately shown, running the whole width of the valley, which was not the case in reality. Also at the time Cardigan reached the smoke, those guns on the Fedioukine Heights had been silenced by the charge of the French Chasseurs d'Afrique.

The charge of the Light Brigade seen from the Fedioukine Heights – note Lord Cardigan leads the charge as they approach the guns. Inaccuracies include the middle row of the 11th Hussars and the number of front row survivors reaching the guns.

Cardigan cares for his men

Much speculation was made subsequently of Lord Cardigan's role in the charge, and whether, like George Custer at the Little Bighorn in 1876 with Major Marcus Reno (also Major Elliott at the Washita, 1868), he abandoned his forces to their fate (see my work *Clearing Reno* volumes 1-5). We shall come to this soon in volume IV. Meanwhile, as the shock of battle and the crushing destruction of the Light Brigade sank in, Cardigan had addressed the survivors of his brigade (his infamous 'Men, it is a mad brained trick, but it is no fault of mine' – see volume II this series).

After this, he attended on the surviving wounded. These had been initially treated in a small church in the village of Kadikoi, situated a mile from the harbour at Balaclava, with the most serious cases taken into the general hospital set up on the port. Here Cardigan visited them and reportedly comforted his injured trumpeter Billy Brittain [7]. The following day, the hospital ship *Australia* with 100 of the most critically injured set off on the four-day trip to the medical facilities at Scutari, near Constantinople (Istanbul).

This was just before Florence Nightingale and her nurses arrived to clean up the place. The hospital apparently had no beds and no bandages – it is absolutely incredible that those who survived the charge would have to recover in a place full of rats and mould covered walls! So much for the recovery of the Light Brigade! It was helped for the less seriously injured in the night of 26th October, when it was reported that about 100 Russian cavalry horses broke free and galloped to the British lines near Kadikoi, causing an alert until it was seen that they had no riders. One animal belonged to a trooper of 4th Light Dragoons killed during the charge, and it likely led the others to the British lines – thus more of the surviving men of the Light Brigade found themselves remounted.

Raglan visits – but not the troops

On October 27th Lord Raglan visited the cavalry camp to speak with their lordships Lucan and Cardigan, but according to Lord Paget, not the surviving troops, which was a shame according to Paget. Raglan was bothered after having spoken to French Commander François Certain Canrobert, who was concerned that his troops surrounding Sevastopol might be in danger of Russian attack now that the effort to seize Balaclava had been thwarted by the British. Canrobert wanted the remaining British cavalry moved up on to the Sapoune Heights to help protect the French armies engaged in the siege of Sevastopol. Lord Cardigan pointed out that such a move would place the brigades seven miles from Balaclava, the British port for supplies.

If the onset of winter made the roads impassable, then no food could be brought up and the danger was of horses starving to death, he surmised accurately. Lord Raglan had already made up his mind on the subject, however. Whilst acknowledging Cardigan's concerns, he ordered the cavalry up on to the heights close to the Inkerman Windmill, and the direction from where any Russian attack might occur. This they did on the 28th; two days later, during strong winds, the first winter snows fell.

Little Inkerman soiree

What made the French commander-in-chief ask for this additional support? At about noon on 26th October, the Russians launched a small attack upon the British 2nd Division (de Lacy Evans, later replaced by Pennefather) on Mount Inkerman, east of Sevastopol. The plan was to divert allied attention away from Liprandi and his army on the eastern side of the Causeway Heights. For this soiree, Colonel Federoff from Sebastopol would lead the attack with six battalions of 4300 men.

Exiting the confines of Sevastopol between the Malakoff and Little Redan forts and then crossing Careenage Ravine, the force moved east before turning south at St George's Ravine and ascending to attack the British 2nd Division in the area of Shell Hill. A second, smaller force of about 700 men also left Careenage Bay area and headed down Careenage Ravine in a pincer movement. Ahead of them all, were just 2644 men (plus some guns) of the British 2nd Division stationed upon Home Ridge, and farther forward around Shell Hill.

On standby to support was Cambridge's 1st Division, George Cathcart's 4th Division, Bentinck's Guards Brigade, and French General Bosquet's men. In the end, as this turned out not to be a major conflict, de Lacy Evans's 2nd Division handled the situation. On the flank, advanced pickets of Codrington's Light Division and some volunteer men from Bentinck's Guards Brigade peered along Careenage Ravine at the advancing Russian right flank; they also had just one Lancaster gun between them.

Additional guns were rushed up by Captain Singleton (these were part of Morris's battery, he having been wounded the day before hostilities began at the redoubts). Shell Hill was manned by advanced pickets from 49th Regiment, and these were able to remain concealed as the main Russian force advanced uphill towards them. Russian movement had been detected earlier by General Codrington, who alerted de Lacy Evans and 2nd Division. As firing commenced, 49th Regiment slowly withdrew from their position to prevent being surrounded by Federoff's main force.

Little Inkerman soiree from Careenage/St Georges Ravine (courtesy Google earth).

Battle commences

Three companies from 1st brigade (also called the Fusilier Brigade, commanded by Major-General William John **Codrington**) were sent forward by their commander, Major **Champion**, towards Shell Hill to support the advanced pickets there, who were by now fighting and withdrawing. Also coming up with the Russian's were some artillery guns; these were harassed successfully by a handful of men under the command of their colour-sergeant – Captain Singleton's batteries thus had time to set their guns up on Home Ridge, ready for action.

At that time, the Russian's made the top of Shell Hill with their artillery, and were able to open fire on British positions on Home Ridge. To this bombardment, eighteen of de Lacy Evans's 9 pounder guns were soon able to respond. The Russian infantry response was to begin descending the slopes of Shell Hill towards the British; here the artillery fire from Home Ridge ceased, for fear of hitting their own men. Major Champion, walking amongst his battling men, repeatedly called to them 'slate 'em, slate 'em my boys!' [8]

Back at Careenage Ravine, just 60 men of Captain Goodlake's Coldstream Guards barred the way across the ravine near some caves. The captain and his sergeant went ahead to be sure that the men would not be ambushed by the enemy; during their brief absence, the Russians suddenly appeared from another part of the ravine - the British fired and began retreating. Goodlake and Sergeant Ashton found themselves cut off from their men. They tried to make good their escape but ran into another mob of Russians, but nobody attacked the two men; they believed later that their almost matching grey uniforms deceived the Russians, and the two British men were able to travel with the Russian force for about half a mile, until it stopped before Goodlake's own men!

The two British officers managed to make good their escape and rejoin their men. The Russian commander in the ravine tried to rally his men to attack the British, but none would go forward, so a stand-off resulted with nobody going anywhere. Meanwhile, Major Champion and companies, earlier fighting towards Shell Hill, had been alerted to the possibility of a Russian counter attack from the area of Quarry Ravine, and took the opportunity to withdraw. This was described as being conducted at a rush. Champion retreated back towards the main line of advanced British pickets, also retreating to the line known as The Barrier, with about 240 men.

British are halted by de Lacy Evans

Champion cautioned his men to charge the advancing enemy, and although some stepped forward, charged and fired, most did not – the enemy, however, having taken a few hits, did withdraw towards their main advancing force on the slopes of Shell Hill. Artillery fire from Home Ridge encouraged their retreat. About this time, Russian commander Federoff was grievously hit. This, along with the steady bombardment from Home Ridge and Captain Singleton's battery, caused the Russians to retreat in full. The British then advanced against the Russian forces, only to be halted 700 yards short of Shell Hill on the orders of de Lacy Evans. In Careenage Ravine the Russians began to retreat when Captain Goodlake's men, reinforced by Captain Markham's men of 2nd Rifle Battalion, saw them off.

Lord Raglan, now aware of the fighting, galloped over from Balaclava and saw Sir George Brown, taking time to personally thank Captain Singleton and Morris's battery for their efforts on Victoria Ridge (which stood next to Careenage Ravine). He then rode off to find de Lacy Evans – by which time, the brief battle of Little Inkerman was concluded. The total length of battle was about three hours (although actual combat time was much less), and the casualty figures were 270 Russian dead or wounded, with 80 prisoners captured including two officers; for the British, 12 killed and 77 injured, with no prisoners lost. The success of the day's events were down to, it appeared, de Lacy Evans's decision to allow the enemy onto ground of his own choosing, and once there attacking them with his artillery pieces – also, letting only a minimal number of 'green' troops gain some combat experience.

3. PRELUDE TO INKERMAN

It is necessary, before continuing the quest to clear Lord Cardigan of any blame for the near destruction of his Light brigade, and for the sake of continuity, to follow events a little longer to and just after the Battle of Inkerman on 5th November 1854.

News from home

On the very same day, Lord Raglan received his usual correspondence from the government back home; amongst communications, to satisfy the contingency in the result of his own sudden death or incapacity, as to a suitable predecessor. The government decided that Sir George Cathcart was the man for the task; whoever decided this had not taken into account more senior men who might take umbrage at the decision. The next senior man after Raglan was Sir John Burgoyne, the engineer, and Sir George Brown.

As a result, only three men were made aware of the government decision: Lord Raglan, George Duke of Cambridge and Sir George Cathcart himself. Such a cock up was swiftly reversed almost immediately by Henry Pelham Fiennes Pelham-Clinton, 5th Duke of Newcastle-under-Lyne, and accepted immediately by Sir George Cathcart. Sir George had been reluctant to accept the new commission in the first place, and Lord Raglan was relieved by the government change of heart.

Another stupid idea

Lord Raglan's next idea was to consider abandoning the Port of Balaclava, due to his shortage of manpower and the danger of General Liprandi seizing the place. For this he was talked out of by Admiral Edmund Lyons, second-in-command of the British fleet, and also Commissary-General William Filder, who confirmed that he could not supply the army without Balaclava Port. Lord Raglan, at another suggestion, ordered as many available men from the navy to be sent ashore at Balaclava to assist in the defence of the port under Sir Colin Campbell. In the end, Sir Colin, along with help from Turkish battalions, the navy, some of Bosquet's men and the whole Highland Brigade, had 2158 men available.

Inklings of things to come

On 2nd November, the Russians under Liprandi were reinforced in the east and thus able to send out warnings to the British. The Russian left was extended to further threaten Balaclava, by extending their forward pickets with artillery protection. The Russian guns just had the range of the British and allied forces facing them north of the port, and this led Lord Raglan to believe the port might be attacked. These Russian reinforcements had taken the long route, from Odessa to Russian Commander-in-Chief Alexander Menshikov near Sevastopol. These consisted of 4 Corps with 10th and 11th Divisions arriving on the 2nd and 3rd November. By the 4th November, the reinforcement was complete, and estimates of Russian ground force strength amounted to between 100,000 and 120,000 men!

The allies, excluding the Turks, amounted to nearly 65,000 men, of which the British had 24,843. The French had 31,000 infantry and the British 16,000 infantry soldiers available. Of the Turks the French had 5000 attached and the British 6000. The usefulness of the Turks was such that Lord Raglan refused to accept any more when offered some by Omar Pasha, their leader. Despite Russian superiority of nearly 2:1, they did not have a sufficient majority to guarantee defeating the allies (3:1 or greater would be required). Perhaps unaware of the build-up of enemy troops in the east from the 2nd of November, General Canrobert, under the guise that his troops were close to breaking the Russian fortress the Flagstaff Bastion, convened a meeting with Lord Raglan for 5th November to discuss a final attack plan. We saw the allied positions around Sevastopol in volume I of this work, but below is another picture of the Russian fortresses to remind us.

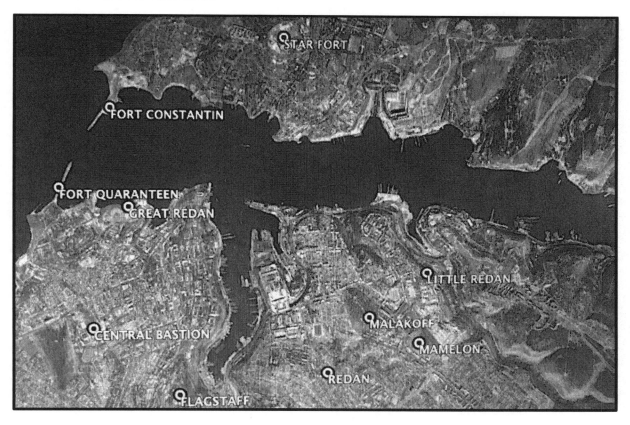

Russian defences around Sevastopol (courtesy Google earth)

Despite the Russian soiree on 26th October against de Lacy Evans's 2nd Division, little had changed in the dispositions of the British on account of the continued siege conditions placed upon the allies. Nobody seemed to think that there could have been another way to bring victory in the Crimea. And now those additional Russian troops in the east were about to descend upon the unsuspecting British and French.

Troop dispositions

The positions of the troops before 5th November was as follows: upon the Victoria Ridge was 1st brigade consisting 7th Royal Fusiliers, 23rd Royal Welch Fusiliers and 33rd Regiment commanded by Brigadier William Codrington (1st brigade was part of the Light Division under Sir George Brown – the other part was George Buller's 2nd brigade). Also up on Victoria Ridge was a naval brigade under Captain Stephen **Lushington** (based at the head of Victoria Ridge) and just one Lancaster gun battery; 2nd division was stationed just behind Home Ridge and likely to take the brunt of any further Russian attack, thus it had pickets extended well to the fore. General de Lacy Evans was not present that day on the 5th as he was ill (he had been injured at the Alma, and some say he had been thrown from his horse earlier), so his next senior officer, Brigadier John Lysaght **Pennefather**, took command of the division's 3300 men and 12 artillery guns.

John Pennefather   *de Lacy Evans*   *William Codrington*

Continuing with the dispositions: whereas Pennefather's 2nd division held the high ground along Home Ridge (approx.194m/636' elevation) and beyond, the Duke of Cambridge (1st Division) had placed his Guards Brigade (Henry Bentinck – 3rd battalion the Grenadier Guards, 1st battalion the Coldstream Guards and 1st battalion the Scots Fusilier Guards) in rear of Pennefather, to protect the Sapoune Heights to the east. Also, Bentinck had Guards Pickets out on a ridge between Victoria Ravine and Wellway Ravine (see maps below). About two miles south of Pennefather's 2nd division was the extreme left wing of the French Army of Observation (Bosquet), which ran along the top ridge of Sapoune Heights towards the junction called The Col, close to Raglan's HQ.

Bosquet had the brigades of Generals Espinasse, deAutemarre and Bourbaki overlooking the plains of Balaclava. Close to The Col, on the road to Balaclava, was General Joseph Vinoy's brigade. Sir Colin Campbell and the Highland brigade north of Balaclava, at Kadikoi (including Marines and sailors of the Royal Navy) completed the main troop dispositions on 4th November. The allied cavalry was stationed near Lord Raglan's HQ close to The Col, but the remains of Cardigan's Light Brigade was camped on the Sapoune Heights close to a windmill.

There were no reserves; all available men were employed during the day and night in the trenches and various outposts and pickets surrounding Sevastopol. Canrobert, French commander-in-chief, would not spare any men for use by the British. The length of the line to be defended in the event of a Russian attack (Balaclava to The Col, then along the Sapoune Heights as far as Sandbag Battery) was about nine miles in length – this excludes all the areas surrounding Sevastopol. Canrobert claimed that all his men were deployed and he was awaiting reinforcements from Greece! He already had 40,000 men (initially) compared to the British, who had 26,000. The extent of the Russians reinforcement was still not known to them.

The day before Inkerman (Allied) north sector (courtesy Google earth).

The day before Inkerman (Allied) middle sector (courtesy Google earth).

The day before Inkerman (Allied) south sector (courtesy Google earth).

Intelligence failure?

Despite whatever Lord Raglan or General Canrobert did or did not do about the build-up of Russian forces to the east, some people in the allied armies did. Some officers received mail from their relatives back home, who in turn received correspondence from Russian friends warning of an impending attack designed to destroy or capture the allied army! Nevertheless, nobody seemed to know that the Russian onslaught was scheduled for 5th November. In Sevastopol, Russian General Moller still maintained an air of defiance towards the allies; he was joined, however, by General Soimonoff (also spelt Soymonoff) and his 10th division, who were to take part in the assault from the port.

His orders were to take his 16,200 infantry (some sources say 18,829) with 38 guns and march up Careening Ravine, ascend its western slope near Victoria Heights, and attack the English centre. Meanwhile, General Pauloff, with 13,500 Infantry (some sources say 15,806) and 28 guns would march from the north side, descend and cross the Tchernaya valley at the head of the bay, before ascending to attack the English right wing at Sandbag Battery; the attack of these two commands would be simultaneous.

Both commanders, Soimonoff and Pauloff, came under General Peter Dannenberg for overall co-ordination. Corps commander General Mikhail Dmitrievich Gortschakoff, with 15,000 infantry soldiers, 4,000 cavalry horse and 40 guns, was to make a false attack upon Balaklava from Tchorgoun area and all roads leading to Sapoune Ridge. General Timofajeff, with some 2,500 men and 4 guns, would make a false attack upon the French left, carrying their batteries if possible. General Pavlov was to bring up reinforcements from the north – various estimates suggest the Russians deployed 100,000 men, although only 68,000 and 235 guns could actually be brought into line to attack. Russian Commander-in-chief Alexander Menshikov took up his base for these operations near the old Inkerman ruins.

Dawn is a feeling

At dawn on Sunday 5th November, the allies in the Inkerman area had 14,200 men. The breakdown of British man resources, pathetic as it was, is as follows – to support Pennefather's 2nd division who were stationed in the Inkerman area: Guards Brigade 1331 men; Light Division 649 men; from 3rd division at Inkerman 281 men and 619 in the Victoria Ridge area; from 4th division at Inkerman 2217 men; British Cavalry 200 – total 5297 men, horse and 26 guns. French forces numbered 3575 men (plus 700 cavalry) with a further 4644 men brought up later. Their gun tally was 24. We must always bear in mind that numbers of men available was fluid and that the majority were still employed surrounding Sevastopol.

Russian initial manoeuvring (white lines) (courtesy Google earth).

Mikhail Gortschakoff   *John Pennefather*   *Charles Bourbaki*

The Russian plan was for 40,000 troops to attack the British 2nd division at Inkerman, coming mainly from the north. There would be 40,000 men against, initially, 5297 British men: a preponderance of over 7:1. More than enough to ensure a stunning and annihilating victory for the Russians. But the opening gambit for the superior Russian forces gathering for the assault did not bode well; it rained almost continuously the day before. With de Lacy Evans sick, John Pennefather was now commanding 2nd division up on the Inkerman Heights. As was his usual habit, he went to the front to look on the enemy positions just before sunset. From the top of Shell Hill, he could see the increasing build-up of Russian troops at Sevastopol; also, the arrival there of a gold coloured carriage which, unbeknown to Pennefather, brought two sons of the Russian Czar to the area to encourage and raise morale of the troops about to engage – these were the Grand Dukes Nicholas and Michael.

Pennefather sent two officers further forward onto the Inkerman 'Spur' to report after dark on any further movement. These men were Captain Carmichael and Major Grant – they reported to him a fresh build-up of Russian cavalry between Tractir Bridge and Inkerman Bridges on the right bank (east side) of the River Tchernaya, but other than this, nothing appeared amiss other than large flocks of sheep seen on the Inkerman Ruins. Throughout the night 'rumbling' sounds were heard from the enemy direction and reported in 2nd division's camp, but these amounted to nothing and no alert was raised. Captain Ewart of the quartermaster-general's department was on early morning dawn patrol and visited each camp site of the various British units to check all was well.

On arrival at 2nd division, the men had just been dismissed following the usual morning muster, but all appeared quiet even at that early hour. Ewart was not the only one active at that time of day; William Codrington of the Light Division, commanding the Victoria Ridge, was likewise up before dawn and riding over to inspect his Lancaster battery gun, where the picket changeover was just taking place. All was quiet as the night duty men began to return to camp. Those men did not get far before being recalled to the battery, as gun fire could be heard increasing rapidly. The battery was manned and the remaining companies took their positions along the Victoria Ridge. Codrington then rode back to camp and alerted the men, much to the annoyance of his commander Sir George Brown, who did not understand at first the reasons for Codrington's actions. Dawn was breaking, and misty too; and the feeling now was that something major was up.

4. INKERMAN EARLY

Alarm is raised

George Brown stopped Captain Ewart, who was returning from visiting 2nd Division, and on learning what was occurring sent him right away to alert Lord Raglan at his HQ. In a very short time, the field-marshal was on his horse and on his way towards the firing. During this initial probing, General Mikhail Gortschakoff on the Balaclava plains prepared to follow his orders from Alexander Menshikov: this was to distract the allies during the main attack by 'drawing them upon himself,' and endeavouring 'to seize one of the routes leading up to the Sapoune Heights' with his cavalry made ready to effect an ascent when it became possible [9]. Gortschakoff left in the early hours his camp at the village of Tchorgoun, where he took position on the Fedioukine Heights in a southerly direction, with his left just in front of the village of Kamara (close to former British Redoubt 1). From here, he began a long range bombardment towards the Sapoune Heights, and moved some of his troops forward in the required feint.

First moves

As the attack got underway, the British moved to support Pennefather and 2nd Division defending the high ground of Home Ridge, Fore Ridge, The Barrier and the Sandbag Battery. The Duke of Cambridge (1st Division) sent some of Bentinck's Guards Brigade forward (Grenadiers, Scots Fusiliers and later the Coldstream) north, to support Pennefather's right flank; an eventual total of 1331 men. Cambridge requested Bosquet send men to occupy the space vacated by the guards; this the French general would not do until things became clearer – a typical French response. It was soon evident that the main Russian attack was at Inkerman after all, and Bosquet then sent battalions forward to the region of the Windmill, where he joined them in person.

At the Windmill, Bosquet came across George Brown and George Cathcart, who actually declined his offer of French assistance, since they believed the English could manage! Not so the wrong decision of Brown and Cathcart for Lord Raglan; he at once reversed their decision by sending an aide, Colonel Steele, to General Bosquet requesting French support up on Inkerman as things were turning serious there. The French general sent 38-year-old Brigadier Charles Denis Sauter Bourbaki, with 2115 men, forward to Inkerman, followed shortly after by more men of the Algerian 3rd Zouvres. Later, he sent General d'Autemarre with 2304 additional men, bringing Bosquet's contribution to 6263 troopers.

Initial British movements

At about 9:30 in the morning, General Timovieff and 3000 men left Sevastopol via Quarantine Bastion and attacked the French on Mount Rudolph, spiking a number of French guns. This attack was to tie down much of the French forces to the west of Sevastopol, who served under General Forey. Involved were Generals De Lourmel, D'Aurelle and Levaillant. The Russians eventually had to withdraw back to Sevastopol, but not before damaging the attacking French forces and killing General Frederic De Lourmel. None of these French troops took part in Inkerman, as they were tied down for too long by the Russians.

Sir Richard England (3rd Division) advanced with 1400 men towards Inkerman – the rest of his division were employed in the allied trenches that morning. On arriving in the area vacated by Cathcart's 4th Division (just ahead of where Bentinck's Guards had also just vacated), he deployed some of his men to hold the ground there, before sending two battalions (1st Royals and 50th Infantry) under John Campbell (his brigade commander) on ahead. He eventually deployed Campbell in such a position to support Codrington up on Victoria Ridge. Cathcart also set off for the Windmill area, followed by 1700 of his men initially, later increased to 2217. General Goldie's brigade consisted 1089 men under Captain Edward Stanley and Colonels Horn and Ainslie; General Torren's brigade consisted 1128 men under Colonels Horsford, Smythe, Swyney and Captain Hardy.

French guns (FG) on Mount Rudolph

General Buller's 2nd brigade (Light Division) was likewise short of men due to trench/picket duty that morning, but nevertheless managed to send up 550 reinforcements for Pennefather (a further 99 men arrived to support Buller later in the day). On the Victoria Ridge east slope was Codrington's 1st brigade, now exposed to the Malakoff Battery guns. An advanced picket on guard in the Careenage Ravine was surprise attacked by advancing Russians, and their officer with 12 men captured. Some Russians turned towards Lancaster Battery in an attempt to seize it, but they were sent running by the bayonets of Captain Elrington and some of his men. General Codrington eventually managed to muster 1219 men, once the trench/picket men had come in from duty – he lost 180 killed and wounded, including two officers dead and eight wounded.

In the fog – early stages

Although separated from Inkerman by about a mile, Codrington could not see Pennefather due to a dense fog then descending around the area. So at around five o'clock in the morning, General Soimonoff, accompanied by about 19,000 soldiers and 38 guns, left Sevastopol and advanced east before turning towards Shell Hill. Using a guide, Soimonoff led in person his troops, ordering the men to keep as quiet as possible so as to surprise the enemy. At St. George's Ravine the joining up with General Pauloff's men did not appear to be taking place. In fact, due to a confusion of orders received from General Dannenberg, Pauloff had still not departed from the area of the Tchernaya River.

Soimonoff did not linger, however, and ordered some of his infantry and guns forward at around six o'clock in silent order. As they headed up Inkerman towards Shell Hill, one Russian battalion lost its way and ended up in Careenage Ravine, where it was, as we saw earlier, able to attack and capture an officer and 12 men of Codrington's pickets. Further British pickets in advance of Victoria Ridge also came into contact with the silently moving Russians. The alert was not raised at the time because the soldier sent from the picket line was captured by the enemy! The 30 men under Captain Goodlake commenced firing, and this alerted Codrington on Victoria Ridge to the problem.

As dawn began to break, the British pickets in advance of Shell Hill could still not see the approaching enemy in the mist and drizzling rain. Several men in the advanced picket location reported the rumbling sounds of carts from the Inkerman ruins area, commencing from around 2 a.m. These were reported to Major Thornton Grant, the duty field-officer. His report raised no alarm back in camp. As was the custom and we have seen already, the men of 2nd Division turned out for inspection on Home Ridge about an hour before dawn; they were then stood down and the usual wood (fuel) and water parties mustered and sent about their fetching duties.

The night duty pickets were replaced by fresh men and sent back to camp. The new pickets took position and all was quiet and still for a time. As the sky lightened, an advanced picket saw what he thought was a Russian column approaching through the mist and alerted his superior, Captain Rowlands. Moving forward, he saw two Russian columns approaching the Shell Hill pickets. The pickets opened fire and the Russian columns turned about and fled; only to return shortly after in greater numbers, and with 22 guns they soon had control of Shell Hill.

2nd Division on alert

The men from the night duty were now turned out again. The 12-gun battery of Captains Turner and Pennycuik were deployed along Home Ridge and ordered to fire into the mist, blind, by Colonel Percy Egerton Herbert. The Russians up on Shell Hill opened up their guns, missing completely the British on Home Ridge but hitting the 2nd Division camp on the south slopes of the ridge, maiming and killing men and horses alike. The camp was of course, almost empty at the time as the men had been turned out. Pennefather, despite a shortage of ammunition at his front, decided to reinforce the small knots of pickets still fighting and still holding back the Russian force at Shell Hill; the main areas of British resistance was the Fore Ridge, the Barrier, and the Sandbag Battery.

Soimonoff attacks (white lines heading towards bottom right)(courtesy Google earth).

Percy Herbert   *Edward Saxe*   *John Mauleverer*

The pickets were reinforced by 30th regiment whilst General Henry William **Adams** took forward 41st regiment; the 49th (Bellairs) moved to the right of Home Ridge whilst on the left of the ridge, the 47th (Fordyce) took up position. The remains of the 95th regiment left Home

Ridge and one wing (Champion) headed for Sandbag Ridge whilst the other (Hume) pushed forward towards the extreme front of the line, where it joined 55th regiment in the fight. The men had to battle mist, drizzle and difficult to traverse brushwood to come within sight of their colleagues, or range of the enemy. These moves, ordered by Pennefather, resulted in but a few hundred men left on Home Ridge to defend it. Once the reinforcing troops had departed into the mist, there was no longer any means of communication with them from Pennefather's HQ.

Raglan near Home Ridge

Lord Raglan allowed Pennefather to continue the battle. The British guns, however, were being out ranged by the Russians on Shell Hill, and so Raglan ordered up two massive 18 pounder artillery pieces. In answer to his first request came the word 'impossible!' but within a short time, the required guns had been hauled up.

On Shell Hill, General Soimonoff had stalled, waiting for General Pauloff and his men to get across the Inkerman Bridge and join the battle. Meanwhile, Soimonoff decided this was the time to attack the British left flank, and so sent forward three columns – one ended up in Careenage Ravine and then the Wellway Ravine, ready to attack the British on Home Ridge.

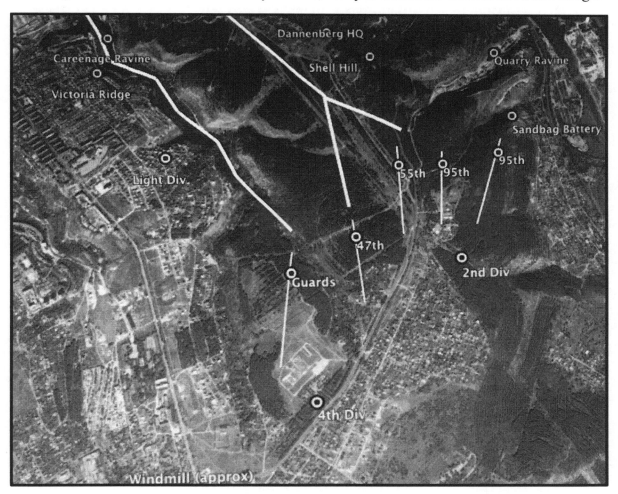

British counter attack (thin white lines with regiment names) (courtesy Google earth).)

British counter attack at Wellway Ravine

During this confusion, a company of Grenadier Guards (Prince Edward of Saxe-Weimar) positioned south of 2nd division as part of Henry Bentinck's Guards Brigade, saw the Russians in Wellway Ravine approaching the exposed left flank of Pennefather, and they attacked the flank of the Russians, who fell back. Soimonoff's middle column, approaching Home Ridge, now split, with one section heading for the Barrier and Sandbag Battery beyond, and the second veering right across Mikraikov Gully directly for Home Ridge. Here they were stopped at a distance of about 80 yards by men of 47th regiment (Fordyce) and the Russians withdrew in disarray.

Shell Hill

At about the same time, 49th regiment (Grant) also near Mikraikov mounted an attack against Soimonoff's middle column. Through the mist, Grant is said to have shouted to his 245 men 'give them a volley and charge,' to which the men under his command obeyed. A fight ensued in which Russian prisoners were captured and Major Grant led his men on foot as far as the Russian guns on Shell Hill. Through the mist, it was clear that Soimonoff was waiting no longer for the arrival of Pauloff, and was advancing in force. A massive group of 9586 Russians began to descend towards the Mikraikov, forcing back Major Grant's men very slowly. Pauloff's men were, however, on the march, and two regiments gained the Shell Hill Heights via Volovia Gorge, in time to join Soimonoff and add an extra 5844 men to the 9586 already there – a total of 15, 430 Russians moving downhill towards the British.

Sandbag Battery

The rest of Pauloff's men came down Quarry Ravine towards the British front at the Barrier. Others turned southeast and headed for the high ground of Sandbag Battery, along with men from Soimonoff's column. Here they advanced with bayonets fixed, only to find the battery abandoned; the seven men of the picket had fled on to the finger spur (known as the Kitspur) to rejoin the rest of their comrades advancing in support (95th regiment). The 95th opened fire on the newly arrived Russians.

Advance to Saddle Top

Now that Pauloff was on scene with 5844 men joining those on Shell Hill and the remainder moving through Quarry Ravine, Soimonoff was able to move his infantry down the slope towards Pennefather's 2nd division on Home Ridge. 24,643 men were thus available to the Russian commander, plus 38 artillery guns perched on Shell Hill. Facing him, Pennefather had just 3622 men and 12 guns of Captains Turner and Pennycuik (plus 6 guns from Townsend's battery: total 18 guns). And the Russians were now fast approaching, through the drizzle and mist, albeit in an unruly line with companies all over the place and mixed. They were approaching Saddle Top Ridge, which lay just in front and to the left of Home Ridge.

British support slain

General Pennefather, riding around Home Ridge, saw 290 men of the Connaught Rangers 88th regiment marching, and ordered them forward, over the ridge and down the slope to join the others. Further units came into action. The 88th came alongside 30th regiment, where their officer asked what was going on. The reply was that there were 6000 enemy on the hill ahead. The Rangers continued on into the mist, however, in a northwest direction along Jut Road, until they could take shelter alongside a stone wall. Here the 'retire' was sounded by bugle, and the men retreated back to Home Ridge. The following day, 16 dead bodies of men from the 88th were found just beyond the stone wall.

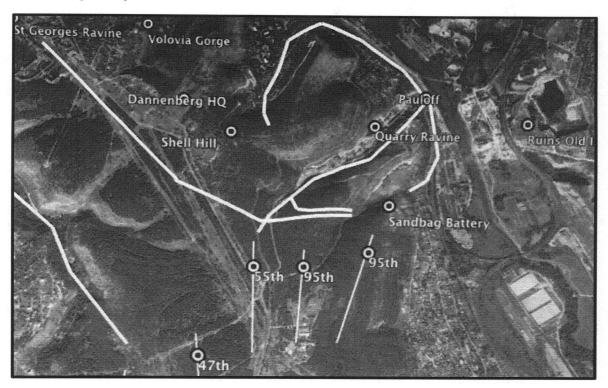

Pauloff arrives via Shell Hill and Quarry Ravine to attack Sandbag Battery (courtesy Google earth).

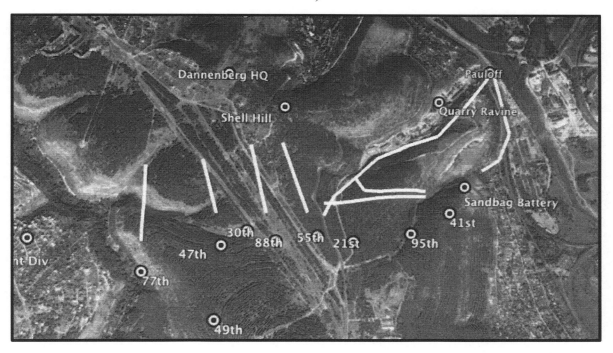

Horns locked (Russians white lines) (courtesy Google earth).

5. INKERMAN MIDDLE

The retreats

Following 88th Rangers came the guns of Major Samuel Townsend's battery, also groping their way northwest in the mist and looking for a suitable place to set up on the Mikraikov Ridges. However, Townsend could proceed no further when they came across the 88th retiring, and there was a real possibility that they would now need to abandon their guns, since the Russians, were close by. Three of his guns fell for a short time, as artillerymen fought hand to hand with the equally surprised enemy. The 88th made it back to the safety, if in disorder, of the British 2nd division camp on the south slopes of Home Ridge. Amidst all this confusion and poor visibility, General George Buller came up to Pennefather's camp, accompanied by his 77th regiment (Colonel Thomas Graham Egerton) consisting 259 men. In the area of Wellway Ravine, the firing of Russian guns could be seen through the mist, coming towards the 77th.

Buller and Egerton did not know that their paltry 259 men were about to face directly 7938 soldiers of the enemy. Nevertheless, Colonel Egerton led his men unsupported in an advance against overwhelming odds; he did not know the Russian front approaching through brushwood and mist numbered 1562 men. The enemy must have seen the British at this time and faltered. Riding on the right side of the advance, Egerton said to Buller 'there are the Russians, general, what shall we do?' to which Buller replied 'charge them.'

Egerton then directed his men to halt, fire, then charge the enemy. The Russians had, however, by this time turned the extreme left flank of the 77th. Buller's aide delivering Egerton's charge message, Lieutenant Clifford, saw this from his horse and rode into the enemy, calling to the left flank company 'come and charge with me.' He then engaged, for which he later gained the Victoria Cross; the men followed, despite the sudden death of their company commander, Captain Nicholson. Losses were high but the 77th regiment fought well in hand to hand combat, led on by their mounted officers until the fight began to move north. Soon, the right flank of Soimonoff's column was retreating back towards Shell Hill. Egerton and his men followed in pursuit.

Death on the hill

The British lay down to avoid the Russian guns firing from the hill, and it was during this phase that General Soimonoff, riding his horse, was shot and mortally wounded. On the British side, General Buller lost two horses shot from under him, and was also badly injured at the same time. About now a rapid advance was made, once the Russians had backed away, to recapture some British guns taken earlier. This advanced consisted of men from 88th, 47th and 63rd regiments, and in little time, the guns had been recovered. At the central column area, Russian forces approached the gun battery of Captain John Turner on Home Ridge, who fired over the heads of British pickets (who were just out of ammunition and retreating).

The destruction was such to turn the advancing Russians, who fled down the slope again, cheered by the British who had been lying prostrate on the ground to avoid being hit.

The men then chased the enemy back as far as the base of Shell Hill. On the right of Pennycuik's guns were now stationed 49th regiment (Bellairs) taking cover and not able to see very much. It became clear soon that most of the British pickets to the front were out of ammunition and retreating.

Bellairs was joined on top of Home Ridge by Captain Adams (aide-de-camp to older brother General Adams), who told him 'I think you had better advance, Bellairs' [10]. To this Bellairs ordered 'fix bayonets' followed by 'advance.' The enemy was just 80 yards away at this stage as the men descended the hill; at 40 yards breaking into a run and cheer before careering straight into the head of this Russian column – the enemy turned and fled rather than fight.

Way out east

We've seen what was happening in the west and centre of the Inkerman Heights, so now to the Inkerman east sector; this being the British area around the Barrier/Sandbag Battery, where upwards of 6668 Russian infantry approached from Quarry Ravine. What they did not know was that they were heading right into General Adams' brigade (this was 3rd brigade (of Pennefather's division) consisting 41st, 47th and 49th regiments). In the area of the Barrier, 1500 of the enemy came into contact with just 202 men of the British 30th regiment. When British pickets gave the alarm, this regiment advanced as two battalions to a low wall near the Barrier: the right wing under Colonel John Thomas Mauleverer, and the left under Major James Brodie Patullo.

The 30th were ordered to open fire, but in those days it was the custom to pile firearms at night outside men's tents, and the stoppers of the rifles in this case had been lost, causing the arms to become wet. The Russians were coming closer and the position became critical; there was a distinct possibility of men becoming nervous. With that in mind, Colonel Mauleverer decided on a bayonet charge, and all officers cleared the stone wall, followed by the men with their bayonets fixed. The hand to hand battle lasted for a few moments before the Russians retreated. During the melee, Colonel Mauleverer was wounded, and in total, 30th regiment lost 31.4% men killed or wounded. But the effect had been to send the Russians fleeing along Shell Hill and Quarry Ravine.

Sandbag recaptured

General Adams was now approaching Sandbag Battery with 525 men of 41st regiment. Passing many retreating pickets who were out of ammunition, they approached Sandbag via the descending Kitspur hill, and were then in line to face 4150 Russians! The enemy started an immediate 'left about' to avoid the British. Retreating in confusion and causing their supporting troops coming up behind to also fall back, the 41st (Carpenter) soon had back control of Sandbag Battery. Adam's did not pursue the enemy. Thus, the British on east Inkerman numbering 3622 men, saw off 24,643 men of the Russian army!

Extra support arrives

So far, Pennefather's 2nd Division had only just held their positions but had lost the high ground of Shell Hill to the enemy. Home Ridge was higher still in altitude, but the mist and drizzle reduced visibility and although the enemy had mainly turned about after the opening salvos, they were not yet defeated. Coming along behind was support from Cathcart's 4th Division and Cambridge's 1st Division. These consisted of 3461 men, plus two heavy extra guns ordered up by Lord Raglan; the time was still early at about 7:30 in the morning.

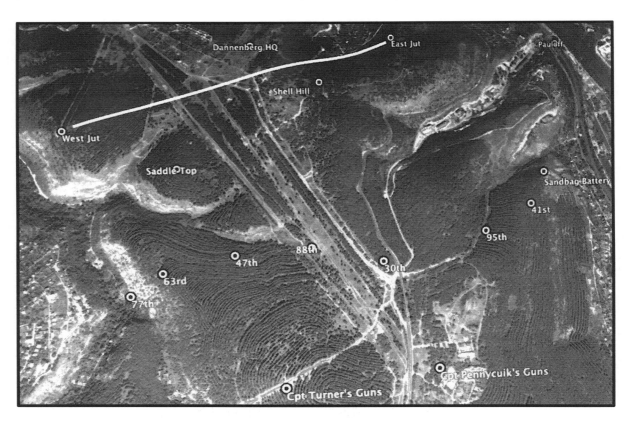

Approximate positions at 7:30; Russian main forces retreat (white line).

At this time, the Russians had 86 guns in along Shell Hill and a mile-long front from West Jut to East Jut. Dannenberg, commanding the lot, had 19,748 men ready around the hill. A lull now preceded the next storm; a lull in which many British soldiers took the opportunity to catch up on some sleep in the damp air, whilst their officers tried to find out where spare ammunition was. General Pennefather had no idea where this could be found either! His advice was that the men should give the Russians the bayonet – an idea also on the mind of French General Canrobert when he went forward to inspect British troops gathered around Mikriakov Spur.

This he deemed very important to hold, and that the men should show their bayonets above the brushwood for the enemy to see! Ammunition was soon brought forward, thanks to the foresight of the Rangers regiment's quartermaster back at camp. On Home Ridge, reinforcements and ammunition finally arrived in the form of 49th regiment (Bellairs) moving in support of the Sandbag Battery; additional artillery pieces arrived (Townsend), increasing the guns on the Ridge to sixteen.

On the reverse slope of the Ridge, regiments were able to retire until needed: here waited the 95th, 55th and 47th. There were, by the time of the lull, 1244 Guards troops supporting the pickets who had already seen action. Captain Goodlake and Prince Edward commanded the pickets, with the Duke of Cambridge in person commanding the rest, including 2066 men from Cathcart's 4th Division. Also on the march were two battalions of French infantry, numbering 1665 men.

Waiting game ends

Despite it being full daylight, mist still shrouded Inkerman Heights as Lord Raglan and his staff sat in their saddles upon Home Ridge and contemplated arrival of the post from home, which duly arrived and was handed out! Even in the midst of battle, the niceties and comforts of home continued to arrive as usual. Opposite the Ridge, at a range of about one mile, General Dannenberg withdrew his initial troops and prepared to deploy fresh troops for the next phase of his attempt to rid Inkerman of the British, and allow free access to the siege Port of Sevastopol. General Adams was near Sandbag Battery with 710 men of his 41st/49th regiments, when the first of Dannenberg's new forces came into view; so large was this force that Adams was forced to send Captain Armstrong, his brigade-major, back to camp to see if there were any reinforcements available.

There he found the guards under Cambridge, and the duke promised immediate support of General Adams, who faced 10,000 fresh enemy troops. To the left of the Sandbag and right of the Barrier, a gap had appeared, called appropriately by General Pennefather, as the Gap. Adams now found the initial skirmishers of the Russian 10th/17th regiments engaging his men. In true sacrificial fashion, when the approaching Russian front line was destroyed by the men of General Adams, fresh lines popped up and replaced them, continuing the advance. Their main effort now poured out of St Clement's Gorge, in an effort to secure the worthless Sandbag Battery. Adams encouraged his men, knowing help was close at hand from Bentinck's guards, as promised by Cambridge.

This led four officers of the 41st to jump up and call to their men to charge the nearest Russians; the officers led by example, but the men did not follow. All four officers were killed on the battlefield; the 41st commander, Colonel George Carpenter, was wounded and finally died of wounds inflicted upon him on his capture by the Russians. Nevertheless, the attacking hordes of Russians soon seized back control of the Sandbag Battery, leaving General Adams and his men to retreat. The enemy, however, did not pursue the retreating British, but did manage to shoot General Adams in the ankle – he died a few months later of his wounds.

The guards advance

As 41st/49th regiments withdrew from Sandbag Battery, an additional three guns (Hamley) joined those already firing from Home Ridge, and the Guards Brigade (Bentinck) with 757 men arrived just behind the Ridge, along with Cambridge himself. The duke was cautious enough to send officers ahead to check the lay of the land before advancing further without Lord Raglan's consent. Charles Russell of the Grenadiers went ahead and reported back that the enemy were 'all around us but thickest there' towards the Sandbag Battery [11]. The guards marched forward, east of the Fore, and then towards the Sandbag, not perhaps aware of the enemy gathered in the Quarry and St Clement's Gorge; 757 men against 7129 enemy troops.

As happened earlier, the damp chambers of the rifles would not fire properly, and as the guards approached the nearest enemy, Colonel E Reynardson ordered the charge by bayonet. The Russians did not wait for the inevitable collision, and ran back the way they had just come. The Sandbag was back again in British hands, and the men had to be restrained from chasing after their foes by their officers; the enemy counter attacked several times later, but to no avail.

Charles Russell

Thomas Goldie

Charles Windham

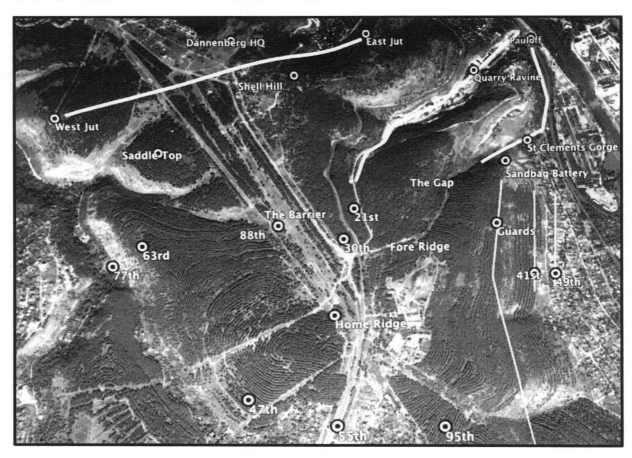

The guards counter attack (thin white line, right. Russians thick white lines) (courtesy Google earth).

The recapture of the Sandbag and frequent Russian counter attacks was enough to send the Duke of Cambridge back to Home Ridge in search of further men. He was able to send one battalion of the Rifles regiment (Alfred Hastings Horsford) and one from 20th regiment (Crofton) to support the Guards up on the Kitspur Ridge (Sandbag Battery). The other halves of these regiments were sent to reinforce the Barrier. Having arranged temporary help, Cambridge rode to George Cathcart and urged him to send troops forward to support the Guards up on the Kitspur. Sir George (not for the first time) refused the request. Further south at Hill Bend stood the French 6th regiment, and further west by the Post Road stood the French 7th regiment. A request for them to move forward in support fell on deaf ears, since their commander, Bosquet, had not yet put in an appearance that morning. This refusal to help their allies caused much resentment amongst British troops.

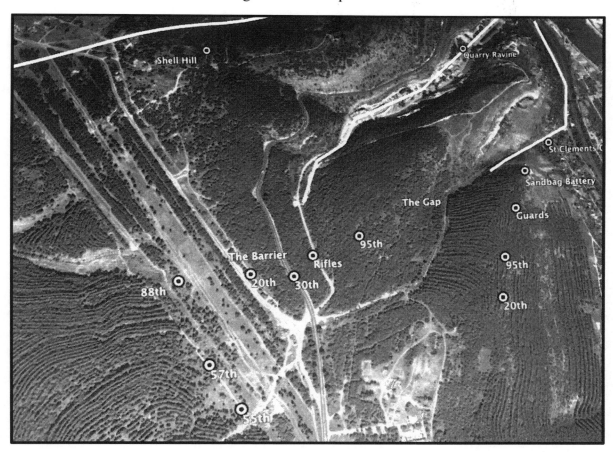

After the lull, approximate locations of various regiments (some were divided) (courtesy Google earth).

Even the intervention of Pennefather failed to move the French forward, and so Cambridge returned to the Kitspur and his stretched troops; the French remained just below Home Ridge – 1665 men idle. Cambridge had secured the support of just 521 extra men.

Russians attack again

No sooner had the duke returned then General Dannenberg decided to launch a heavier attack against the British, preceded by a heavy bombardment from Shell Hill and East Jut upon the Kitspur. Then, 7129 Russians began an assault on the Sandbag Battery area, where the British gave way again and took refuge on slightly higher ground but from where they could attack the advancing Russian masses. But Russian command of the Sandbag was not to last very long; for, with the Coldstream Guards approaching from the south the Grenadier Guards, almost out of ammunition, commenced a bayonet charge led by Colonels Henry Percy and Charles Lindsay that resulted in the Russian occupiers turning and fleeing once more.

With the threat of a massive Russian counter attack, it was time for General Pennefather to distribute Cathcart's 4th division reserves; these Cathcart had already put at Pennefather's disposal with the 21st Fusiliers (Colonel Fredrick George Ainslie – 201 men) and 63rd (Colonel E. Swyny – 368 men). They took position on the very far left of Home Ridge; to the right of the ridge at the Post Road was a group under General Thomas Leigh Goldie (a 20th regiment wing under Colonel Horn with 180 men and the 57th regiment under Captain Edward Stanley with 196 men). General Arthur Wellesley Torrens was approaching too, with 46th regiment (Captain Hardy) and 68th regiment (Colonel Henry Smyth) with a total of 384 men.

Cathcart's folly

So far we have seen French regiments not moving forward towards the Kitspur in support of the Guards around the Sandbag, and the appearance of a spot called the Gap, between the Barrier and St Clement's Gorge just below the Sandbag. This needed plugging to allow a cohesive front, and George Cathcart was now in a position to assist. Lord Raglan sent General Airey with an order to Sir George, who was by this stage up on the Kitspur with his men firing into the gorge below at Russians. Airey had the men cease firing before he could deliver the order: Sir George was to move to the left and support the brigade of Guards and not to descend or leave the plateau; those were, he added, Lord Raglan's orders.

Sir George was inclined initially to move from the Kitspur and attack below the left wing of the advancing Russians, along St Clement's Gorge, but now he was being diverted to another part of the battlefield albeit only about 400 yards farther. Nevertheless, Cathcart did not appear to question Raglan's order but instead ordered Brigadier Torrens to attack. In doing so, Torrens would need to descend the Kitspur with his 384 men, contrary to Lord Raglan's order to not descend or leave the plateau. The 4th Division moved down the Kitspur towards the Russians; Brigadier Torrens at the head of the 68th and 46th with George Cathcart and staff following behind. Because of an earlier order by Sir George to remove their greatcoats, his force was mostly dressed now in conspicuous red uniforms. Russian artillery shells fired from East Jut at the discernible red uniforms began to land close by.

6. INKERMAN LATE

Death descending

Brigadier Torrens was shot and fell wounded, and Sir George rode over and said to him 'Torrens, well and gallantly done!' [12] Torrens was removed from the battlefield and died several months later of his injuries. All around the Kitspur and the Sandbag, British troops had to be restrained from charging down the slopes towards the encroaching enemy in the gorge below; ammunition was becoming low again and hand to hand battles started everywhere. George Cathcart, descending the gorge, heard firing just behind and looking back saw columns of Russian soldiers who had crossed the Gap unopposed, and were doing battle with the British up on the Kitspur.

Sir George had not, of course, reached or secured the gap but now found himself with Russians below as well as above. Sending Colonel Windham of his staff ahead to try and bring back as many of Torrens's men as possible, Cathcart managed to assemble some fifty nearby men of the 20th regiment. He decided to attack the enemy above him. The ascent back from whence they had just come was difficult and tiring, but about half the men managed to get to the level of the enemy force. Most of the Russians gave way and fled at the sudden appearance of the British. Others, however, did not. The British, outnumbered about 14:1, could not disperse the enemy, and Sir George and staff, riding just below the wavering assault, deemed themselves in trouble.

'I fear we are in a mess,' he said to Major William Maitland of his staff [13].

Maitland rode down a way to encourage up some troops, who complained to him that they had been fired upon by their fellow troops on the slopes above (in fact, they were Russians). The ascending troops stopped because they had no ammunition left anyway, so Maitland turned back and rode up towards Sir George and his aide, Colonel Charles Seymour. Both men rode forward towards him when the enemy struck all three; Sir George Cathcart was killed instantly with a musket ball through the heart, as was Charles Seymour, with Maitland seriously wounded. The Russians were reported to have bayoneted both dead men's corpses many times [14]. Another killed about this time was General Thomas Fox Strangeways, commanding the Royal Artillery, who had a leg blown off whilst riding up to Lord Raglan and who passed away an hour later from blood loss; his horse survived the explosion.

Confusion near Sandbag

Another senior officer finding himself in trouble was the Duke of Cambridge, operating near Sandbag Battery, according to Kinglake [15]. He like Cathcart suddenly found Russian troops above and below him, and was technically cut off. Against him was estimated to be 2000 of the enemy, whereas the duke had about 150 men. The duke was warned by his staff that he would be taken and that it was the Russians firing at him. The Russian troops were now so close that it was surprising Cambridge and his staff managed to make good their escape close to the head of Quarry Ravine.

During this manoeuvre, the duke lost his horse and was shot in the arm by enemy fire; with the help of some straggling guardsmen he and the others made good their escape. The Russians also turned about, for approaching their right flank came the French 6th battalion from the area of Hill Bend, and the Russians descended towards the head of St Clement's Gorge. Thus Cambridge was shortly afterwards reunited with his missing Grenadier Guards survivors. French 6th battalion, although hesitant at times, finally reached the Sandbag just as the Russian forces fled down St Clement's Gorge.

Counter the Rifles, 63rd and others

Near the barrier, the troops, mostly of the 30th regiment, were forced back by fresh Russian regiments coming down Shell Hill; until they eventually joined their colleagues up on Home Ridge. This led General Pennefather to order the Rifles (the left wing) near the Barrier to attack the approaching Russians. Just 140 riflemen, descending the slopes of Home Ridge, turned back a largely superior enemy force who mostly fled into Quarry Ravine. There, the Russian survivors regrouped and attacked again, this time meeting 200 men which were part of 95th regiment under Major Hume.

On some parts of Home Ridge, Russians actually got to the crest in the mist, unopposed, until it was realized they were not British. The 30th were resting there when the enemy suddenly appeared, and it was necessary for the exhausted men to jump up and chase the enemy back down the slopes once more. Up on the Kitspur, Cambridge sent Colonel George Upton and two companies of Guards to try and plug the Gap; upwards of 3000 Russians in two columns were seen approaching from Quarry Ravine. Ahead of Upton, some British soldiers were seen engaging the enemy (likely the 95th and the Rifles), but soon after Upton's Guards were forced back as far as the sanctuary of Hill Bend by enemy pressure.

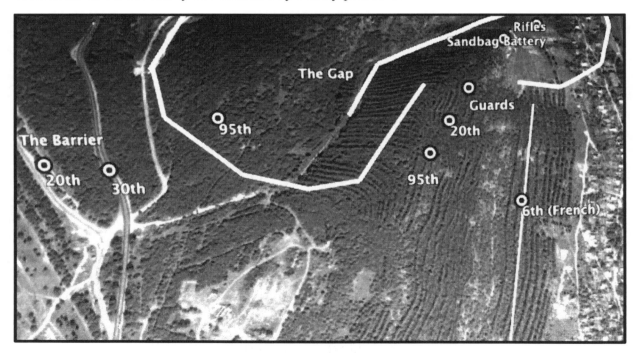

French (thin white line) finally move forward and take the Sandbag (courtesy Google earth).

To the west of Home Ridge, three guns of Boothby's, attached to Turner (on the left of the Ridge) were sent downhill to the far left by Colonel Fitzmayer, because of increasing Russian pressure. General Pennefather was forced to ride down to Colonel Swyny of the 63rd and the colonel was ordered to charge the enemy the moment they appeared. The remains of the regiment discharged one volley as the enemy approached the British guns, and then charged with bayonets fixed. On their left, Colonel Ainslie's 21st regiment also joined in the attack. The result was that the enemy turned and fled, chased by the two regiments until they came within range of the Russian guns on Shell Hill, where the British withdrew.

The 20th and 57th succeed

Approximately 1500 yards to the east, two wings from 20th regiment (Colonel Horn with 180 men) and 57th regiment (Captain Stanley with 196 men) moved forward under Brigadier Goldie, on Lord Raglan's orders, and descended to the right of the post road from Home Ridge. These found large Russian forces ahead, and fired on them, causing the enemy guns up on Shell Hill to send artillery pieces at them. The 20th, however, charged down the slopes of Home Ridge and bayoneted the enemy. The Russians gave way and were in disorder as the survivors of the 20th advanced as far as Quarry Ravine. Enemy guns appeared in the area of the East Jut, and fired upon those around Quarry Ravine.

The British used marksmen, who took aim at the guns, causing the enemy to rapidly remove their weapons. The 57th regiment under Captain Stanley who were approaching, saw a Russian column coming up Home Ridge, and likewise charged the enemy. The Russians fled, before turning to fight hand to hand; during this, Captain Stanley was mortally wounded and Captain Inglis, taking command, saw off the enemy back into Quarry Ravine. Thus about 376 British troops saw off 2000 Russians from Home Ridge to the Quarry. Both the 20th and 57th regiments then retreated back onto the top of Home Ridge and kept up a steady fire that stopped any further Russian advance. A lull in the action now followed.

Dannenberg takes stock

Back near Shell Hill, General Dannenberg must have taken stock of things; he had 100 guns still on the Hill, stretching from West Jut to East Jut, plus 9036 fresh troops out of view of the British. The allies were in a sorry state, following the early morning battles, with most units reduced to just a few hundred men if that. Against Dannenberg's impending new attack, the British had but 3300 men available, including some still unsupported French troops – 1000 men were on the largely un-attacked west slopes. This was all about to shift shortly.

Sometime after 8:30, Dannenberg committed the next wave of his battle; vast Russian columns exited Quarry Ravine and Shell Hill, heading towards Home Ridge in a rush. Pennefather, in command of the defence of the ridge, could not see the enemy leaving Shell Hill because of gun smoke; those further down the slopes could see. The main enemy thrust was from Shell Hill, east of Saddle Top, and ended up close to the Barrier. There they supported those emerging from the Quarry and the whole mass, approximately 6000 Russians, advanced towards Home Ridge. At this stage in proceedings, just 590 British under Pennefather stood on the Ridge, with a further 259 approaching from 77th regiment under Colonel Thomas Graham Egerton.

Boothby's guns

A surprise flank attack, hidden from view and separate from the main central Russian advance, swept around and succeeded in surrounding Captain Boothby's three guns on the lower west slopes of Home Ridge. A fierce hand battle ensued, with the few British soldiers taking hits including a gun commander, Sergeant Major Henry, who received no less than twelve Russian stab wounds but survived! The enemy quickly spiked the guns with wood. The guns did not stay in Russian hands for long, however, for a troop of about 60 French Zouaves arrived in time to recapture the British guns; these often unruly men went into the attack off their own volition, against the orders of their higher commanders.

Almost defeat on the east slope

As the guns were recaptured by Zouaves, farther east the 57th and 55th regiment remains came under surprise attack from Russians who appeared out of nowhere; many British were captured and marched back again towards enemy lines – but the enemy, however, did not relieve the men of their weapons, and after a brief fight, many of the captured escaped. The Russians continued to advance towards the crest of Home Ridge; just west of the post road near the top stood three of Captain John Turner's guns, who discharged 'case round' at the enemy before withdrawing the guns to avoid capture.

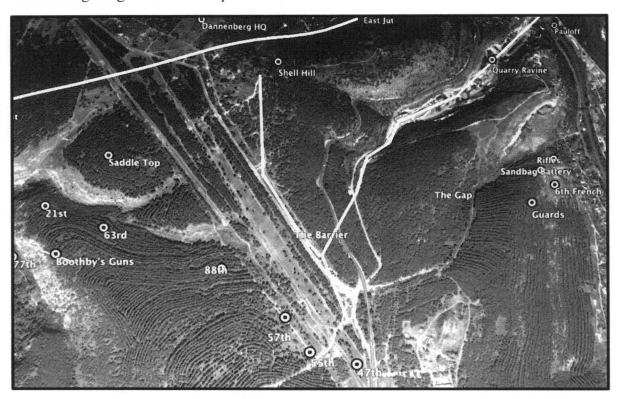

Approximate allied positions at the end of the lull (thick white lines Russians) (courtesy Google earth).

Thus the Russian vanguard, pouring over the crest of Home Ridge, saw before it in the distance Pennefather's camp, and were also unopposed by the British. But not for long; the French 7th Leger regiment had just left the British camp site and were headed up the hill, directly towards the Russians. Not for the first time, the regular French faltered when they saw the enemy coming down the hill towards them. Only the timely intervention by a mounted British officer, shouting in French, spurred them on towards the Russians. Supporting them on the right were the survivors of 77th regiment led by Colonel Thomas Graham Egerton, who had earlier withdrawn from the far left of the line near Wellway Ravine.

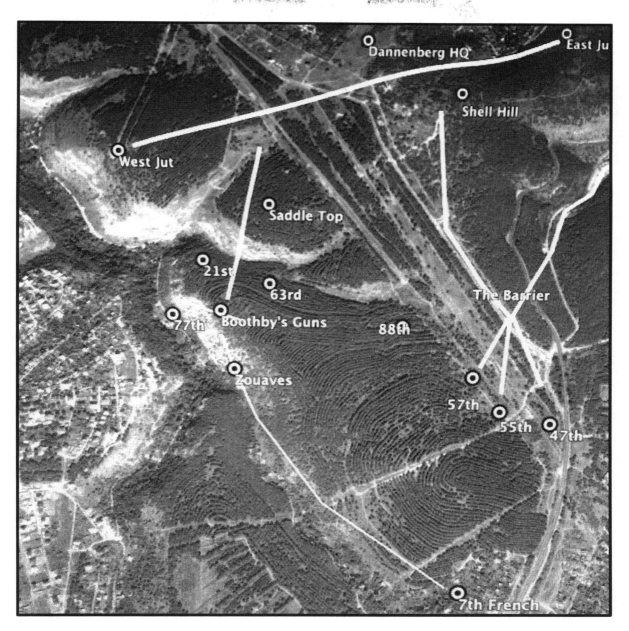

Zouaves recapture Boothby's guns (courtesy Google earth).

However, as the French came closer and closer to the enemy they turned once more and retreated down the slope, leaving Egerton and the 77th exposed and alone. Lord Raglan was incensed when he saw the French begin to retreat, and sent an aide to the reforming and battered 55th regiment to prepare them to intervene. It was about now that General Thomas Fox Strangeways, commanding the Royal Artillery, had his leg blown off whilst talking with Lord Raglan, and needed assistance to get off his horse. At the same time, Raglan's exposed location led to other members of staff losing their horses but fortunately not their lives.

Colonels Somerset and Gordon being the most noticeable of them. On the reverse (south) slope of the ridge, the 55th under Colonel Warren, charged the enemy and took up hand to hand fighting. After a short time, the Russians withdrew and the British retook the ground lost. The French had been halted in their advance and turned about, with support of Egerton's 77th, and soon the Russians in the centre post road area had also retreated over the crest of Home Ridge.

The enemy advances again

There were still around 2000 Russian soldiers in the centre, ready to commit to battle, and seeing how their vanguard had gone over the ridge before retreating again, they advanced to the foot of the ridge and began to move up once again towards the British and French survivors. Pennefather was joined by a French officer and 60 Zouaves who had previously saved Boothby's guns on the western slopes, and these were deployed on the up slope, just east of the post road approach between 57th regiment and the faltering French 7th regiment.

Down near the barrier, the main Russian troops (the previous being the advanced vanguard of the enemy) were approaching and held at bay by Colonel William Bellairs and the remnants of his 49th regiment (and others). Perhaps he could not see the size of the Russians, but others could, and a field officer was dispatched who ordered Bellairs to retire immediately. The colonel reluctantly ordered his motley bunch to retire at the walk, continuing to fire on the approaching enemy until they had all but run out of ammunition. Bellairs managed to extricate about 200 men from the various regiments from the Barrier.

7. INKERMAN END

The French hold the line

The ammunition-less men under Colonel Bellairs, including some from 20th regiment, hastened their retreat when the commander of the advancing French 7th regiment warned that they were about to open fire upon the rapidly advancing Russians. The enemy began to drop but continued slowly up the slope of Home Ridge, where the firing French started to falter again. But any retreat was precarious, for standing directly behind them was Bellairs and his survivors from the 49th/20th regiments. Shouted commands of encouragement from Pennefather and his staff close by and above them, stopped the French 7th from retreating, and so continued their firing upon the Russian columns.

On the left of the French line, Colonel Henry Charles Daubeney with 55th regiment remains went ahead and attacked the Russian 2nd battalion, which had been following the first. There followed a melee with men on both sides locked together, unable to bring weapons to bear and using only their fists and boots. The 55th broke through and came out on the east side of the Russian advance; the French 7th with supporting Zouaves and British began to advance once again against the confused enemy.

Forget not the British left wing

Recovering on the far left of Home Ridge near Boothby's guns waited the 21st/63rd regiments facing generally northeast. These now began to advance in that direction, until reaching the post road, where they turned north to confront the enemy. At the barrier, the Russians fought and held ground against the British before finally fleeing along the Post Road and into Quarry Ravine; yet still nobody was safe, for the 63rd regiment's Colonel, Exham Swyny, fell from his horse killed by a rifle ball wound to his head. Also hit was his adjutant, Lieutenant Robert Bennett, who was severely wounded and his horse killed. Colonel Fredrick Ainslie of the 21st also received a fatal wound at the Post Road whilst gathering some men to dig a defensive trench.

Another lull

The enemy withdrew, but a stalemate ensued with at least 9000 Russian troops still uncommitted and Shell Hill, East Jut and the West Jut still in their hands; and the time of day was still only about 9:15 in the morning, according to *Kinglake*. Lord Raglan had not one fresh unit available at that time with which to pursue the enemy and take the initiative; what he did have was adequate ammunition supplies held at 2nd Division's camp just below Home Ridge. As the lull commenced, men were sent back to camp to replenish supplies. Reinforcements under French General Pierre Bosquet had finally arrived, albeit a little too late; their attempt to chase and engage the Russians was quickly stopped by firing from Shell Hill.

On the allied right flank, near Quarry Ravine, the 6th French regiment began to retreat under Russian pressure, and their commander, Colonel Edmond Jean Filhol de Camas, was badly injured and captured by the enemy, where he later died from a chest wound. The 7th French regiment was positioned with the 6th, but both regiments were turned by the enemy and a staff officer sent to General Bosquet requesting immediate reinforcements. There were none available; strangely, the Russians did not follow up the retreating French, and so the high ground near the Sandbag area was not given up.

The area around The Barrier was prepared for any further attack from Quarry Ravine, and pickets kept careful watch upon Shell Hill for any sign of Russian movement. And that movement soon came – not from Shell Hill, but from the mouth of Quarry Ravine towards The Barrier once more. The advanced pickets retreated, and Major Ramsey Stuart of the 63rd regiment was ordered back by General Goldie to 2nd Division camp, to gather any spare men, including the camp's guard; there, he found 150 exhausted men who he ordered forward. More stragglers were picked up on route and joined the command.

Frederick Haines   *Collingwood Dickson*   *Lord West*

They were soon at The Barrier under Colonel Frederick Haines, defending it against the advancing Russians. They were joined soon by a company from 77th regiment under Lieutenant Acton, who moved in advance to the mouth of Quarry Ravine before it was forced back to The Barrier. Another company from 49th regiment under Lieutenant Astley also joined to reinforce Haines and Acton. General Goldie received a fatal wound at about this time – senior officers on horseback were always easy targets for enemy soldiers [16].

18 pounder siege train

With the British clinging on to The Barrier and Home Ridge, another miscommunication of Lord Raglan's orders inadvertently brought forward a two gun, 18 pounder siege train under Colonel G Gambier. The shells of the Russians were by now bursting thickly among the camp of 2nd Division, so Gambier was ordered to get up two heavy guns (the 18 pounders) on the rising ground of Home Ridge and to reply to Russian fire, which the light allied guns were utterly inadequate to meet. The men had to haul the weapons up into position, as no horses were immediately available – Colonel Gambier was injured and handed command over to Colonel Collingwood Dickson. They took position up on Home Ridge, to the fore, facing Shell Hill.

Sometime around 9:30 the first gun opened fire, falling somewhat short of target, but the result was that the second shot became deadly accurate in hitting the enemy on Shell Hill – they had not the same size cannon with which to respond. Lord Raglan joined Dickson's 150 men in watching the bombardment. The enemy response started to wane and their lighter guns were quickly being moved in an effort to avoid contact with the 18 pounders. A dozen French guns soon joined the British on the Fore Ridge, and laid heavily into the confused Russian gunners on Shell Hill. General Bosquet had with him 450 men of Bourbakis' Chasseurs a pied, followed by 1500 men from D'Autemarres brigade including 3rd Zouaves. Everything told, there were about 3764 additional soldiers.

Get stuck in the French

General Bosquet wanted to make a quick survey of the battlefield in front before committing troops in support of Lord Raglan; the French Chasseurs a pied veered off to the right, towards the Sandbag Battery and their countrymen from 6th and 7th regiments – the remainder were ordered forward towards the now retreating Russian columns. Coming up in support were D'Autemarres' men, including French cavalry (Chasseurs d'Afrique) and bringing up the rear (to all our surprise) the British Light Brigade (the decimated brigade still had five regiments, but just 200 mounted men at this time – it was commanded by Lord George Paget, for Cardigan had overslept it appeared on his yacht).

During manoeuvring, the brigade lost five further men killed and five wounded. The French meanwhile moved forward, with two guns brought up and prepared to fire. Bosquet himself went ahead with his staff to peer down Quarry Ravine, to where he presumed (erroneously) the British held control – only to find Russian troops moving towards his position! The guns prepared again to move, but one was captured by the enemy and taken into Quarry Ravine – it was later recovered by the French. Bosquet and staff fled on horseback, unmolested by the Russians. Fresh Russian soldiers in the area of St Clements Ravine were seen heading towards the Sandbag Battery once more.

Here they saw French troops gathering, and so veered to the right to engage them. To the far left of the French line, more Russians from the Quarry Ravine area forced the French to retreat as far as the British lines on the Fore Ridge. During this, the British were advised by their French counterparts to withdraw, since the French could not hold their line. Dickson with his two 18 pounders, remained firm. The Chasseurs d'Afrique, brought up to the Fore, also came under Russian cannon attack and retreated.

The Light Brigade likewise followed to safety. Why the French began to withdraw is not entirely clear, as they had not lost many men at all by this stage of the battle, and furthermore, the Russians had not taken up their advantage of turning the French and pursuing them. All was not lost, however, for the rest of D'Autemarres' troops had arrived (numbering around 2304 men) and Lord Raglan, although without reserves, found himself joined by troops sent by Codrington over on Victoria Ridge – these were 225 men under Major Wilton from 50th regiment, plus 151 men from 57th regiment under Captain Stanley.

Bosquet determined to recover the lost ground of the Kitspur, and so sent forward his Zouaves and Algerines once again. Near the Sandbag Battery, the French managed to liberate the remains of 95th regiment, who found themselves cut off by the enemy – the French were also joined by men of the Coldstream Guards, who had been operating on the wooded slopes of the ravine. The Sandbag Battery was recovered with much Russian bloodshed, and the allied flag flew once more. Those Russians able to escape moved down the slopes and across the water viaduct, clear of the battlefield; the exhausted 95th retreated back to Home Ridge.

The French 6th/7th regiments, who had gathered by the Post Road, were ordered forward by Bosquet towards the Barrier; here the British simply sought cover behind piles of rocks and shot down any Russian advance. It was now 11:00 in the morning and the battle, as we have seen, had been ebbing and flowing back and forth all morning through fog and mist, with the Russians gaining ground only to be dislodged a little later by the undermanned British forces.

The French finally came into their own, but by elevenses they had made their final moves at this stage of the battle.

A state of affairs

Lord Raglan must have by now surveyed the precarious position of all his command, and felt that defeat was not likely. General Canrobert had troops placed just behind Home Ridge in support of the British there, with even more ranged from The Fore to The Kitspur. As for the British, they still had much force guarding Careenage Ravine under William Codrington, with the remainder from Home Ridge to The Barrier and Sandbag Battery. Canrobert, wounded slightly in the arm, was with Raglan on Home Ridge when the latter decided to send an aide to Pennefather to enquire of 2nd Divisions state. Pennefather reported to the aide (Captain Somerset Calthorpe) that an opportunity to finish the battle was presenting itself to the allies if only for lack of reinforcement.

The message that with such reinforcement the allies could 'lick them to the devil' was reported to Raglan and Canrobert by Calthorpe [17]. Pennefather was sent for by Lord Raglan; he reported that he felt the enemy was beginning to yield and also that he had more troops than he believed. Canrobert was not so encouraged by Pennefather's report, and suggested that since the French now commanded a larger portion of the allied front than the British, that a truce be held between the French and the Russians! Lord Raglan, quite rightly after such loss and bloodshed, did not agree, and whilst the French were to hold firmly the ground gained so far, the British alone would continue the battle against the Russians until the enemy had been defeated.

The British move on

At the front, Collingwood Dickson's two 18 pounder cannon had almost expended their ammunition (100 rounds each!), and more was rapidly brought up. During the wait for fresh ammunition, the commanders on the ground at the barrier were making further plans to finish the battle once and for all by taking out the western most batteries up on Shell Hill. Charles Richard Sackville-West (soon to be 6th Earl De La Warr), also known as Lord West, commanded part of 21st Fusiliers. Near Mikriakoff Gulley (just below West Jut) and towards The Barrier, he came upon Lieutenant William Molesworth Cole Acton of 77th regiment, with about 50 men.

Lord West pointed out to Lieutenant Acton the Russian guns on the far west side of Shell Hill that were firing close to their position, and told him to take some additional soldiers under his command and 'advance against the battery.' They must take the battery, or drive it off. The additional men were pointed out to Acton by Lord West, but their officers pointed out to Acton that they were understrength and could not comply with a flank attack upon enemy guns. Acton said that he would act alone then, with just the 77th, but even these men refused to follow, since the other officers present thought it not possible due to the understrength companies.

After a short time one man (Private James Tyrell) from the 77th joined Acton, followed by another, until before long the entire 77th lined up behind their officer. Dividing his men into three sections to flank the guns, Acton ran up the slope with his men. The other understrength companies rapidly followed. With the British 18 pounders now firing at the same enemy guns, the Russians sent in their horse teams to take them away; the enemy managed to withdraw all their serviceable guns on the west side of Shell Hill. By the time Lieutenant Acton reached the top of the hill, he was not the only British soldier there in position.

Lieutenant Astley with 49th regiment was approaching, as was Colonel Alfred Hastings Horsford (Rifles Regiment). By one o'clock, Russian General Dannenberg gave orders for the army to withdraw from the battlefield. This was noticed on various parts of the battlefield, including General Codrington up on Victoria Ridge (Careenage Ravine) who was able to see the Russian guns being withdrawn and sent John Miller Adye with a message to Lord Raglan. Meanwhile, the Russian regiment covering the withdrawal from Shell Hill disobeyed orders and began to charge down the hill again towards the British.

They quickly turned about, however, when Collingwood Dickson's two 18 pounder cannons fired at them, killing and maiming many more Russian soldiers. Lord Raglan debated whether to pursue the enemy, and maybe even seize Sebastopol as a prize, but Canrobert and his French army of the Crimea, numbering 41,786 men and with this jewel sparkling not far away, refused to attack. Thus the British did not follow up because of their lack of manpower, although the artillery did bombard the enemy to ensure their withdrawal. Later, Canrobert regretted that he did not permit his army to follow after the Russians.

John Adye

The Russians go

The Russian commander-in-chief, Prince Menshikov had handed executive command of the battle to General Dannenberg at the beginning of hostilities, and throughout had remained at St Georges Ravine but a five-minute ride from Dannenberg. Now that he saw Russian troops withdrawing, he came out to suggest stopping the retreat on a line with Malakoff battery on the east side of Sebastopol. Dannenberg would not stop the retreat, citing that his men had exhausted their power and his artillery were completely undone. Menshikov ordered Dannenberg to stop the retreat, but Dannenberg replied that to do so would result in the men being killed to the last man. If it was to be so, then Menshikov should give the order to halt himself. To this the commander-in-chief said nothing, and turning his horse, galloped back from whence he came. The Russian retreat once started could not be stopped. Part of the defeated army headed back towards Sevastopol, and part of it headed down St Georges Ravine then eastwards to cross Inkerman Bridge. Others used the Quarry Ravine, all the time harassed by British artillery fire. Eventually, only two Russian guns fired down at Dickson's 18 pounders, and this forced Lord Raglan to order a ceasefire; the result of this was that the Russians were finally able to remove their last guns. General Canrobert managed to secure the East Jut, where his guns were able to harass retreating Russians until Russian ships in the harbour began to fire at the Jut; causing the late arriving French to cease their fire. By three o'clock, the battle for Inkerman was over.

8. AFTERMATH OF INKERMAN

Casualties

Canrobert and Raglan were able to ride out together to East Jut and survey the situation for themselves. Both men became aware of the number of Russians they had defeated; Canrobert of the number he had allowed to escape. The day had been saved, it appeared, by Collingwood Dickson and his two 18 pounder guns. To the gunner Lord Raglan said 'you have covered yourself with glory!' [19] The dead and dying lay around for as far as the eye could see. The last of the Russian guns being dragged away reached the safety of Sevastopol by around eight o'clock in the evening. It would be next to impossible to determine the number of casualties on either side by this stage of what must have been one of the bloodiest battles of recent times.

The Russians lost most men during the battle, as was to be expected; but a preponderance of 3:1 is usually considered enough to guarantee crushing any foe and the Russians certainly had that figure when hostilities commenced on the morning of November 5th 1854. Lord Raglan believed he had been up against 40,000 Russian troops; the real figure (including cavalry but excluding artillery guns) was between 53,500 and 68,000 men. Against them were around 14,200 allied forces, many of whom were just coming off night shift in the trenches surrounding Sevastopol.

The Russians lost about 10,729 killed, wounded or captured – their official return suggests 2988 dead, including 6 generals and 256 officers. For the British, there were 2357 killed or wounded, with 597 dead including 39 officers with 91 officers wounded. Five generals were killed: Brigadier Strangeways (artillery), General Adams (died later of wounds), General Cathcart, General Goldie and Brigadier Torrens, with 10 generals wounded or disabled. By contrast, the French listed 25 0fficers killed, along with 150 men and 1530 men wounded [20].

Recrimination

Lord Raglan assembled a court of inquiry shortly after the battle to ascertain what happened and what went wrong during Inkerman; also, atrocities appear to have been committed. An offer of truce was made to Menshikov so that the dead could be buried; he replied that it was the duty of the side that had possession of the battlefield to do that, and so the allies buried 4400 Russian war dead. Crimes against the wounded by Russian troops were considered; there were numerous cases where the enemy had bayoneted to death wounded or dying allied soldiers at the urging or non-intervention of colleagues or officers. Why should the Russians do this? One excuse was that most of the troops, prior to battle, and being of quite strong religious beliefs, had been consecrated by blessings and prayers calling for blood!

During truce negotiations, Prince Menshikov said that any such injured or disabled soldier would be under the protection of the Russian imperial flag (like a sort of early Geneva Convention), but during the heat of battle, some soldier might do an act of violence that was to be deeply regretted. The Russian commander-in-chief doubted, however, that such atrocities had really been carried out by his men because they must have been provoked by religious sentiment! He went on to say that his countrymen were religious but may have been horrified when they found out that a holy church had been desecrated by the invaders of their country.

Here Menshikov refers to the Holy Church of St Vladimir near Quarantine Bay at Sevastopol, which had been pillaged by the French! It could be seen clearly from the defences around the town by the Russian soldiers. French General Elie Frédéric Forey denounced this as, on the other hand, groups of injured Russian soldiers often feigned death before opening fire upon nearby allied troops. The allied series of advanced pickets (in trenches) worked well as an early warning system during the Russian attack at Inkerman; the only problems it seems was that the attack occurred at the 'change over' period, thus the relieving allied troops were fresh and those headed back to their tents tired, plus the fact that the allies completely underestimated the number of troops the enemy would commit to battle.

How the allies' won

A summary of how the allied forces beat the vastly more numerous Russian army would take many books to fill! But I shall condense it quickly before we move on briefly as to what happened during the remainder of the Crimean war, and then clearing Lord Cardigan from blame for the debacle that was the charge of the Light Brigade. On arrival in the Crimea, the allies were perhaps (and certainly the British) ill prepared for what was to come. Lord Raglan was in overall command, but he was not in a position to dictate to his French allies – we should remember that thirty-nine years earlier, we had been at war with them (Trafalgar, Waterloo, etc.). The first French commander (Armand-Jacques Leroy de Saint-Arnaud) appeared not very co-operative; at the Alma, the first major battle of the Crimean war, his troops were slow to respond when the British attacked, even though they had easier ground and fewer of the enemy to attack.

Despite the allied victory against inferior troops (the Russian army was not as complete as it was at Inkerman), the French would not move rapidly after the Alma to seize Sevastopol, as Lord Raglan wanted. As a result, the opportunity was lost and the allies instead were forced to take control of Balaclava Port and surround Sevastopol. The bombardment of the town followed, which did not dent the besieged Russians who were still able to reinforce their garrison and block the port so that the allied navies could not sail through. The town was also bombarded from the sea by the allies, with the French navy changing plans at the last minute without consulting their British counterparts.

Next we come to Balaclava, and the attempt by Liprandi to take the port by the Russian army. This was stopped by a few British troops and guns after our allies the Turks, who controlled the forward redoubts, had fled the scene. The battle continued with misinterpreted and confusing orders from the British commander-in-chief, leading to a clash of personalities on the battlefield and the debacle that we know today as the charge of the Light Brigade. It was preceded by the charge of the Heavy Brigade in defence of Campbell's 'Thin Red Line.' In all this, the French committed just the Chasseurs d'Afrique cavalry on the left flank of the Light Brigade (who had by now advanced down the valley of death) and up onto the Fedioukine Heights, where at least they were able to reduce artillery casualties as the Light Brigade retreated.

The day after the charge, the Russians launched Little Inkerman, which seems to be a probe into British positions around Careenage Ravine, Shell Hill and Home Ridge; a precursor to their main attack of the 5th November. During this, the British lost 12 men killed and 77 injured. Then we come to the battle proper for Inkerman. If the Russians had succeeded, there can be little doubt that the allies would have had to abandon operations in the Crimean

Peninsula. But it was not to be. The reason can be best described as follows: the ground was unsuitable for manoeuvring large bodies of men, horses and artillery; the foggy and damp conditions of the morning made co-ordination difficult, and effected the cartridges (when they became damp) of both sides; the suicidal way the enemy attacked in mass, leading to vast bloodshed and lastly, the quality of both officers and men on both sides.

Most historians would probably say that the British officers ranked well above those of their Russian counterparts, and this was probably true. Many officers, however, obtained their rank simply because they could afford to purchase their commission; having money does not necessarily mean that those making the purchase were officer material. We only need to look at the bickering between our Lordships Lucan and Cardigan to see the smouldering resentment and jealousy amongst senior officer ranks. Then one might ask who back in London placed these two men together – under arms and in command of hundreds of men? The British middle officer ranks and juniors fought without doubt with bravery and minds set on the task in hand. The senior officers were often found wanting.

Some senior officers, such as De Lacy Evans, suggested to Lord Raglan that the allies abandon the siege of Sevastopol; this his lordship rejected immediately, primarily because the allies had just lost over 2500 killed or wounded men in the battle of Inkerman. The effect of De Lacy's suggestion was that Raglan sent correspondence home pleading for every available man that could be sent. It was no wonder, for at the start of battle the Russian infantry regiments averaged 2619 men and officers each, whereas the British averaged 492 men and officers. The British had about 7464 men in the field at Inkerman with 200 cavalry and 38 artillery guns (includes the two 18 pounders). Our French allies had about 8219 men in the field at Inkerman, plus 700 cavalry and 24 artillery guns. The Russians committed 71,841 men in the field with 271 artillery guns.

Army Operation in Victorian times

The layout and command of this important department and the Victorian British army was, as to be expected, soundly complicated! There were no fewer than seven independent authorities in the organisation of the Victorian army. Like the actual army itself, there was a severe muddle, duplication and mutual jealousy between departments. The commander-in-chief, based at Horse Guards, was a chief of the Imperial General Staff and so in command of all troops in Great Britain. He did not command those sent or based overseas. The Master-General of Ordnance was in charge of equipment, fortifications and barracks; also, the Royal Artillery and Royal Engineers with respect of pay and discipline. There was a Board of General Officers who took charge of all military clothing.

The Commissariat, of which William Filder was a member, was a civilian authority and department of the Treasury that took charge of supplies and transport. In fact, it had very little effective means of moving supplies and no actual transport (thanks to economy cuts) – local transport had to be paid for, as we have seen during the allied landings at Kalamata (or Calamita) Bay! The Purveyors Department, which was a subsidiary of the Commissariat, supplied the Medical Department with some but not all of its requirements. The army Medical Department was independent of other departments, except that the Secretary-of-State for War financed it.

The Secretary for War also looked after the pay and finance of the army, except the Artillery and the Engineers, and also made arrangements with civilian contractors. His department was not responsible for the size and cost of the army, however, which came within the province of the Secretary-of-State for the Colonies, who was also the Secretary of State for

War! As if this tangled web was not complicated enough, many commanding officers considered their regiments as their own personal property and would ignore or evade instructions and rules coming out of Whitehall. Their attitude was entirely understandable. An Army List printed a scale of regulation prices for commissions.

It showed, for example, a lieutenant-colonelcy in a line regiment costing £4,500 (today about £368,000); a cavalry regiment £6,175 (£505,700); the Household Cavalry £7,250 (£593,700) and the Foot Guards £9,000 (£737,100) in Victorian money! No wonder the senior officers had to be very comfortably rich! Officers knew, however, that commissions were often sold for prices in excess of these; popular regiments could change colonels for as much as £40,000 (£3,276,000) and on one occasion £57,000 (£4,668 000)! Having paid so much to command a regiment, the officer might not feel inclined to allow too much interference in his running of it, and was allowed by Queen's Regulations a remarkably free hand.

We have seen above the purchase prices for senior officers in the British army around 1854 – there was no inflation as we know it in those days, so prices remained much the same throughout the century. For the more junior officers, there were two methods of entry: commission purchase, or by recommendation without purchase – the latter purchase had to be approved by the regimental colonel, and the former method required vacancies to be or made available. Lord Cardigan was reported to have purchased his 15th Hussars for between £25,000 and £35,000 – today the equivalent of £2,047 000 and £2,866 000! How the rich lived, and with the common soldier earning just 1 shilling a day (10p = shilling, or £18.25 per year), from which food and lodging would have been deducted.

The most junior officer in a Royal Horse Guards Regiment was the cornet, who purchased his commission for £1200 (£98,280) and received an annual pay of about £71 (£5815). To receive the next rank of lieutenant he would need to pay £1600 (£131,000) to earn £94 (£7698). A captain would pay £3500 (£286,600) to earn £206 (£16,870) and a major £5350 (£438,100) to earn £350 (£28660). The colonel earned about £427 a year, or about £34970 in today's money. The Life Guards regiments earned slightly more as lieutenants or captains; Dragoons less as cornets or lieutenants; foot guards considerably more for captain and major in particularly, and line regiments considerably less than all the others listed here.

Purchase for an ensign (replaces cornet) was about £450 (£38,850) to earn just £27 (£2211) a year. Prior to the Crimean War, there were two types of army promotion, as mentioned: army promotion (or brevet), and regimental promotion. Regimental promotion could only be obtained without purchase when such vacancies existed, usually due to death (war casualties) or if additional officers were required. The rules of promotion by purchase was when a vacancy occurred in a higher rank of the regiment (that was usually by retirement of an officer selling his commission), every officer had claim, according to their seniority, to purchase the next higher rank, assuming that the colonel and the commander-in-chief did not object.

It was also the practice of the army that an officer who was able to pay the cost of the commission would not be passed over by another in the same regiment, unless he had committed poor conduct; thus, no officer was promoted without purchase over the head of his senior in the same regiment. Such was the life of a typical Victorian army officer.

Winter approaches

Now that Inkerman was over, Lord Raglan had to consider planning for the rest of the war, and also the impending and fast approaching winter. Just three days after Inkerman, he instructed the commissary-general to prepare for the army to winter in the Crimea. This man was 64-year-old William Filder, who was shortly to be severely criticized by both public and army alike.

William Filder   *James Estcourt*   *D. of Newcastle*

He reported directly to an assistant secretary at the Treasury back in London, in this case, Sir Charles Trevelyan. Assisting Filder initially were 40 men. Their task is often underestimated, and in today's army individual departments carry out the tasks formally done by these civilian civil-servants. The tasks of Filder's commissariat included meeting the expenditure of the army and keeping costs to a minimum – just like today, and there was not a limitless chest from the treasury. The tasks of the commissariat included pay, food (including horses), fuel, lighting and land transport (including the movement of guns), clothing and ammunition to name a few.

Also included was removal from the field of the sick and wounded (the dead we must assume were buried where they fell, or in mass graves or cemeteries). In the field, the men of Filder's commissariat wore military uniform and held military styled rank befitting their status within their sphere of work – ranking from brigadier down to ensign. Without a dedicated army transport corps, it was necessary, as we have seen previously (Vol I), for the commissariat to obtain transport locally in the country of occupation for the movement of foods, forage, fuel and timber. After that, it was necessary to supply the army by sea – and there was a shortage of this especially as winter approached.

A shortage of fast steam ships was also a thorn in the side of the commissariat as it sought out supplies of vegetables and meats from Turkey and its neighbouring countries. Another problem appeared to be the inefficiency of the only British port in the area: Balaclava. It became necessary, following Inkerman, for Raglan's engineers to build extra wharves so that more ships could be accommodated at any one time.

Of roads and horses

Lord Raglan also made a decision to reinforce (with stone) the main road from Balaclava to the Col, and hence British HQ and the army camps; this was because the dried mud track would likely turn into a quagmire when the winter rains fell. Naturally, he could spare few troops so 400 men of the Turkish army commenced the construction. The total road that needed construction was about 4 miles long.

Ordnance supplies of varying size (unknown).

Its build was not helped by having to transport much of the rock from other locations, and the bad weather setting in, including a storm on14th November. Work on the road was not helped by the rains, which prevented the use of wagons, and the use of horses and mules was likewise impeded by lack of fodder for the animals. Filder had arranged for hay to be sent over regularly from England, since the Turkish type was deemed unsatisfactory; now bureaucracy at home started to rear its ugly head at the treasury board querying why Filder asked for 2000 tons of hay (his communication of 13th September) [21] to be sent to Constantinople.

The board believed the region of the Crimea where the allied armies had just landed to be rich in resources. The treasury board decided to wait for further communication from Filder – this was dated 22nd September and duly arrived on 9th October. Although there was much fodder in the region, he announced, there was no guarantee of delivery from the local population because Russian cavalry was close on the heels of Raglan's advancing army (from the Alma to Sevastopol).

The board wrote back to Filder, announcing that steps would be made to deliver the hay depending upon his subsequent reports to them – one full ship was sent, however. As the end of November approached, just 270 tons of hay had been sent. Appeals from William Filder subsequently sent the board into action, although the quantity being sent was never sufficient. The tonnage was poor and nowhere near that required in one load, but spread out as far ahead as February 1855!

9. THE INQUIRY

Raglan intervenes again

In December 1854, the commissariat was removed from control of the treasury board and handed over to the war department instead; the Minister for War (Duke of Newcastle) also failed to use his vast authority to make sure the hay was delivered in time for the winter months. We see now that as winter commenced, most of the horses of the British army were in all likelihood about to starve. And what of the men? They were nearly in the same dire position: 1½ lbs of bread or a 1lbs of biscuit daily, 1lbs of meat or salt meat, coffee and sugar when available, rice or barley and free shots of spirit for those on the night shift or picket duty. The coffee issued was of the green variety, which needed roasting prior to use; okay when there was sufficient fuel (wood) with which the men could roast the beans, but otherwise useless. Meat rations declined during winter. Lord Raglan tried his best with the commissariat to send up supplies of fresh vegetables for his men from the British base at Varna.

Further, he ordered from the treasury, as a matter of urgency, bread making equipment (a steam mill and bakery). Lime juice to prevent scurvy, was ordered in also by Raglan – incredibly, it was never issued as routine along with the soldier's food rations. Following a storm on 14th November, many of the men's tents had been destroyed, and provision of replacements from home was made by Raglan – these alone took months to arrive, although his lordship found additional provision from the island of Malta. As if that was enough, Lord Raglan sent commissariat officers to Constantinople and other Turkish ports to acquire timber, nails and the tools necessary for the construction of winter huts for the men. The stuff arrived promptly at Balaclava port, but as was to be expected, not enough transport horses and men were available to ensure rapid dispersal of the timber.

Of sick and wounded

Another serious problem mainly afflicting the British was the poor state of the medical facilities for wounded or sick soldiers; there was no ambulance service in the field, unlike the French army. Initially and very surprisingly, there was no provision at all for recovery of the sick or wounded – regular soldiers and sergeants had to be used as nurses until help could be sent from home! The main British hospital as we have seen (in Vol I) was at Scutari, looking across to Constantinople, and run by Major Charles Sillery. Before too long, shiploads of injured and sick men were being transferred from the battlefields of Balaclava.

Sillery was the commandant and had sole military charge of all British hospitals; Doctor Menzies was superintendent of all the hospitals and Doctor Hall, the Inspector-General of the Army, was sent by Lord Raglan to inspect all hospitals in October 1854. He reported them to be in as good a state as could reasonably be expected, but the apothecary's department at Scutari was in no better condition either. In the barrack hospital of Scutari during November 1854, there were about 2000 patients and the number of shirts washed was only six!

Florence Nightingale, at the suggestion of the Secretary-at-War back home, organised a band of nurses to travel to Scutari and undertook the care of the sick and wounded. A fund was raised by public subscription and administered by the owners of the *Times* newspaper. By these means, much suffering was greatly alleviated at the hospital and the spirits of the men raised with many more lives saved. There were actually two hospitals at Scutari – the general and the barrack, which were not far from each other. By the end of November 1854, after the battles for the Alma, Balaclava and Inkerman and with the siege of Sevastopol still on going, there were over 3,000 men in those two hospitals.

There was no attempt made to separate the ranks or regiments, although the wounded were kept separated from the sick – these being men with cholera, dysentery and fever. Even a few wounded enemy troops received the same treatment as the British! As early as 23rd October Lord Raglan had written to the Duke of Newcastle saying that his army needed to rest; and this was before the charge of the Light Brigade, Inkerman, and the onset of the approaching winter!

Storm clouds

We've already mentioned a storm struck Balaclava on 14th November and the destruction it caused was described as a hurricane or even a tornado. It was followed by driving snow. It caused the loss of several French warships, but the centre of danger must have crossed Balaclava port, for the British lost no less than 21 ships, mostly anchored off shore, with 8 damaged severely. That of the land was equally destroyed, including housing, tents and trees up rooted. Food stores for both soldier and horse likewise were lost. Men were found frozen to death in their tents; those few tents that were still standing.

But the loss of stores on those ships, along with their men, would be most keenly felt immediately after the storm. No less than 10 million rounds of one type of ammunition (Minie rifle) was lost on *the Resolute,* who was the primary British ammunition ship of the day. The loss of 20 days' worth of horse fodder was to be serious, as was only to be expected. Lord Raglan got on replacing lost items immediately the storm abated; the commissariat was active right away in Constantinople looking for blankets and suitable warm clothing for the soldiers. Sickness casualties of course rose alarmingly, as did the loss of horses and mules; there was no point, Lord Raglan must have surmised, replacing horses when so much hay had been lost during the storm.

Cold sufferings

The effect of the actions of Lord Raglan and the commissariat quickly brought relief to the men of the British army – not so relief for the horses and mules upon which the army relied. The French had a much better system and suitable warm clothing for their soldiers was already stockpiled by the end of November. The shortage of fuel with which to make fires was a problem for all the allies: the Russians suffered 25,000 sick, wounded or dying and to the allies, frostbite was a serious illness maiming many men. The French lost much of their cavalry horses as well as the horses used for pulling artillery and transporting supplies and ammunition to the battlefield.

They also suffered great casualties of sick or wounded in their field hospitals, numbering 12,238 alone in March 1855, with 11,458 deaths in a six-month period. Scurvy was in much abundance too, no thanks to the poor diets of the soldiers – 23,250 during the whole campaign! But the French did have reinforcements arriving. These came from France and other parts of the French empire; by March 1855, Canrobert had 95,000 men in his army! The British were in dire straits too, for the lack of transport was debilitating the supply of food and warm clothes from Balaclava – it appears that it was down to each regimental commander to procure transport with which to collect items for his men.

This was the job of the commissariat to arrange, but they did not; colonels used their own officer's horses, amongst others, to try and collect the necessary things. The required blankets and clothing was down there at Balaclava port, only many regiments could not collect them! Dead horses lay where they fell since nobody had the strength to remove them; camp cleanliness, or lack of it, was becoming a breeding ground for further sickness. In February 1855, the British had 13,608 men hospitalized out of a meagre force (compared to the French) of 30,919 (44% of the force). [22]

Between November 1854 and February 1855 a total of 8898 soldiers died in British hospitals. Occasional British reinforcements arriving quickly found themselves reduced in number, due to sickness and naturally, the true state of the British army in the field was soon reported home by journalists attached to Lord Raglan. The obvious danger here was that the Russians would find out and use the weakness of their enemy to launch another Inkerman or Balaclava.

Winter of our discontent

Back in England, the Duke of Newcastle was compelled, as public opinion wanted to know why the British army was suffering so much in the winter, to begin apportioning blame on his suffering charges abroad. Correspondence soon arrived in the chilly office of the equally suffering Raglan: that there was no system or organization out there; that there was carelessness amongst the higher departments, and lastly, that such inattention of the army was the responsibility of Raglan's adjutant (Airey) and adjutant general (Estcourt). Official communications in January called for the removal of these people – the scape goats of the disaster that Whitehall was partially responsible for, and trying to cover their backs. Lord Raglan would not have it; unless Newcastle recalled him from duty, then he had full confidence in both men! Dissatisfaction about the course of the war now arose rapidly in England. Reports detailing the mismanagement of the conflict caused Parliament to begin investigations, and on 29th January 1855, John Arthur Roebuck MP introduced a motion for the appointment of a select committee to enquire into the conduct of the war. After discussion in the House of Commons, the coalition government under Lord Aberdeen resigned when Roebuck's motion was voted by a majority of MP's.

John Roebuck MP   *Lord Palmerston*   *Lord Panmure*

Lord Palmerston (Henry John Temple, 3rd Viscount) formed a new government, and John Roebuck headed the eleven-man inquiry into the Crimean war. Fox Maule-Ramsay, 11th Earl of Dalhousie (Lord Panmure) became new Secretary of State for War (replacing

Newcastle). There were some casualties in the Crimea; Sir John Fox Burgoyne, head of the British engineers, was recalled in February 1855 – he was replaced by General Sir Harry David Jones.

Harry Jones

William McMurdo

John McNeill

What was described as a 'land transport' service system was to be set up immediately under Colonel Sir William Montagu Scott McMurdo. Two new commissioners, John McNeill and Colonel Alexander Murray Tulloch, were sent to the Crimea to check out the commissariat system. Other commissioners were sent to report back on the state of the British hospitals and military camps; Needless-to-say, the shortage of hay for the horses was resolved and shortages sent right away. Lord Panmure still insisted, by correspondence in February 1855, that Lord Raglan's staff should be changed, to satisfy public opinion back home. General James Simpson was also sent out there to look into the composition of the general staff surrounding Raglan, and to report any changes he felt necessary. Simpson eventually reported back to Whitehall that there was not one general staff officer that he wished to see removed, and that there was no better selection of officers.

Alexander Tulloch

James Simpson

Aimable Pelissier

Board of inquiry

John Roebuck's inquiry took about a year to complete, and asked more than 21,400 questions of witnesses. Originally Roebuck wanted the inquiry to be held in secret, but this was rejected. Some of the findings of the Roebuck report follow now in shortened form, and the conclusions are fairly obvious. But there were also 'animadversions' (criticisms) of some senior officers (Lucan, Cardigan and Airey), and these will follow in more detail in the final concluding volume. After we have examined briefly the board of inquiry, we shall look quickly at the final battles of 1855, the death of Lord Raglan, and the end of the Crimean war.

Condition of our Army before Sebastopol

An army encamped in a hostile country 1630 miles from England (in a direct line) and engaged during a severe winter in besieging a fortress which, from want of numbers, it could not invest, was necessarily placed in a situation where unremitting fatigue and hardship had to be endured. The inquiry committee were, however, of opinion that this amount of unavoidable suffering has been aggravated by causes hereafter enumerated and which are mainly to be attributed to dilatory and insufficient arrangements for the supply of this army with necessaries indispensable to its healthy and effective condition.

In arriving at this opinion, the committee made allowance for the unexpected severity of the storm of 14th November, and they have not been unmindful of the difficulties which a long period of peace must inevitably produce at the commencement of a campaign. From 16th September, when the army landed in the Crimea, until the end of October, or, as some witnesses state, until the middle of November, the troops suffered from over-work and from dysentery, but were not, upon the whole, ill provided with food.

Even at this period, there was a want of clothing for the men in health, and a painful deficiency of appliances for the proper treatment of the sick and wounded. From the middle of November, this army was, during a period of many weeks, reduced to a condition which it is melancholy to contemplate but which was endured, both by officers and men, with a fortitude and heroism unsurpassed in the annals of war.

They were exposed, under single canvas, to all the sufferings and inconveniences of cold, rain, mud, snow, on high ground and in the depth of winter. They suffered from fatigue, exposure, want of clothing and insufficient supplies for the healthy and imperfect accommodation for the sick.

The Conduct of the Government at Home

The general direction of the war was in the hands of the Duke of Newcastle who, in the spring of 1854, held the office of Secretary of State for War and Colonies. In July, the Duke was relieved of colonial duties and undertook the immediate conduct of the war. When this important change was effected, it does not appear that any order in council, minute, or other document was prepared, defining the special duties of the War Department.

The duke, as Secretary of State, had ample powers; he states, however, that he felt his means to be insufficient for the due performance of his separate duties as Secretary of State for War; he considered the organisation of all the war departments and their relation to each other to be in an unsatisfactory state, but he felt it to be impossible, consistently with attention to pressing business, to attempt their re-organisation.

At the date of the expedition to the east, no reserve was provided at home adequate to the undertaking. The order to attack Sevastopol was sent to Lord Raglan on 29th June; the formation of a reserve at Malta was not determined upon until early in November. When Newcastle informed Raglan that he had 2,000 recruits to send him, he (Raglan) replied that those last sent were so young, and unformed, that they fell victim to disease and were swept away like flies. He preferred to wait. In December, the power of reinforcing the army with efficient soldiers was so reduced that the government thought it necessary to introduce a foreign enlistment bill for the purpose of raising a foreign legion.

The Transport Service in the Black Sea

Sir James Graham said that the naval commander-in-chief, Vice-Admiral Dundas, had authority over the whole of the transports; Lord Raglan had a concurrent authority over this service. Vice-Admiral Dundas, on the contrary, alleged that he had nothing to do with the transports. According to his assertions, they were entirely under the management of Lord Raglan, Rear-Admiral Boxer and Captain Christie. In Balaclava, there was a division of authority: the transports were under the immediate direction of Captain Christie; the harbour was under the management of another naval officer and the shore was subject to military authority.

Commissariat in the East

It is the duty of the commissariat to furnish the army, when in the field, with provisions for the men, forage for the animals and land transport. The military system in this country affords the commissariat no opportunity of becoming acquainted with the army, or of ministering to its wants. In a campaign, the officers of this department find themselves called upon to furnish supplies in regard to which they have had no experience. The officers and men, being often ignorant of the proper duties of commissariat, consider the department responsible for everything they may require.

Land Transport

From the first, the system of land transport was found to be imperfect. No adequate measures were adopted for its improvement, so that the army, when encamped before Sevastopol, depended for all its supplies upon a service defective in its organisation and in its superintendence.

The Road

So much of the suffering of the troops has been ascribed to the wretched, or as some witnesses stated, the almost impassable condition of the seven miles between Balaclava and the camp, that the committee endeavoured to ascertain who was responsible for the maintenance of the roads, and what insuperable obstacles impeded their repair. When the army reached the heights above Sevastopol, they found two principal roads from Balaclava to Sebastopol, one the fine government road called Woronzoff road, and the other, farther to the left, a useful farm road. The army held the Woronzoff road up to the time of the battle of Balaclava. Immediately after that action, it became necessary to draw in the outposts, which lost to the army the use of that road; the other road, however, remained, and was available for all purposes until the rains commenced.

On 13th November, Commissary-General Filder wrote to the quartermaster-general, expressing his apprehension and calling attention to this important subject. The duty of making and maintaining roads for the army falls upon the department of the quartermaster-general. This officer was about this time disabled by severe illness. Sir John Burgoyne, the chief engineer officer on the staff and other military authorities, stated that the soldiers could not be withdrawn from the trenches for the repair of the road.

The men were already overtasked by military duties; they were growing weaker from day to day while their difficulties were increasing. An attempt was made to employ Turkish troops on this work, but it was soon abandoned. From 14th November, the date of the hurricane, the land-transport was gradually reduced in strength, until it almost ceased to exist. The commissary-general writes 'the men and beasts perished owing to the fatigue they underwent in struggling through the deep mud with supplies, and from exposure to wet and cold.'

As far as the information obtained enables the committee to form an opinion, it appears to them that in this matter there was a want of due foresight and decision. The probable failure of the communication was not, however, brought to the notice of the Duke of Newcastle until too late to enable him to take measures in England to prevent the serious calamities which subsequently arose.

Food for the Men

The witnesses were not agreed as to the quantity of fresh meat supplied to the army. Vegetables, which according to the intentions of the government should have been issued gratuitously, were very scantily supplied. Indeed, several witnesses assert that none were ever seen in the camp. Coffee, ordered as an extra ration, was distributed to the troops in a green state and (there being no means of roasting it) was of little use.

Forage

When the army first encamped before Sevastopol, stacks of forage were found in the neighbourhood; these were soon consumed. After the hurricane, the supply of forage failed and under the combined effects of work, exposure, and insufficient food, the cavalry gradually ceased to exist as an effective force. To what extent the commissariat is responsible for the deficiency in all these supplies, is a question to which it is not easy to give a definite answer. Sir Charles Trevelyan, speaking as head of the commissariat and desirous of relieving the department of responsibility, affirms their conduct throughout to have been irreproachable and ascribes blame to other persons.

Medical Department in the East

The army, when sent to the east, had a greater number of medical men in proportion to the troops, than ever before accompanied a British army, and the witnesses generally concur in testifying to their zeal and efficiency; many of these were, however, disabled by sickness. The condition of the tent-hospitals was, from 28th November to 23rd of January, was so wretched and painful to hear that the committee gladly avoid repeating these deplorable details. The medical men, it is said, were indefatigable in their attention; but so great was the want of the commonest necessaries, even of bedding, as well as of medicines and medical comforts, that they sorrowfully admitted their services to be of little avail.

Hospitals at Scutari

Major Sillery was commandant and had sole military charge of the hospitals. Dr Menzies was superintendent of all the hospitals. Dr Hall, the inspector general of the army, was sent by Lord Raglan to inspect the hospitals in October. He remained at Scutari about three weeks and then reported them 'to be in as good a state as could reasonably be expected.' In justice to Dr Menzies, it must be admitted that he was engaged in incessant and onerous duties; the duties of Dr Menzies were further obstructed by a conflict of authority with the purveyor, who claimed to act independently, under the instructions of the Secretary-at-War. The committee must declare it to be their opinion that blame attaches to Dr Menzies, in as much as he did not report correctly the circumstances of the hospital.

When it is remembered that the insufficiency of these stores was a source of much suffering, if not of more fatal results, it must be observed, that heavy responsibility attaches to the commander-in-chief of the forces, who, acting on the representation of the quartermaster-general, retained Mr. Ward in his office after he had been pronounced unfit to discharge its duties. The apothecary's department at Scutari was in no better condition. When the quantities of hospital stores which were sent from England are contrasted with the scarcity, or rather the absolute dearth of them at Scutari; and when the state of the purveyor's accounts is remembered, it is impossible not to harbour a suspicion that some dishonesty had been practiced in regard to these stores. In order to show the dreadful discomfort of the men, and the neglect on the part of the authorities, it may be sufficient to state, that in the barrack hospital of Scutari, during the month of November, while there were about 2000 patients in that hospital, the whole number of shirts washed was only six. The want of an energetic governing authority, with an adequate staff to maintain constant inspection and efficient discipline, appears to the committee to have been the chief cause of all the evils: 5,000 or 6,000 men, although in hospital, require the care, superintendence, and control of an efficient general officer as much as the same number in the field.

Mr. Herbert says that 'Major Sillery worked very indefatigably in his department, according to his own light, but that he was not a man of the rank in the army and the weight which he ought to have had, to be at the head of an establishment of such a gigantic character.' It may not have been possible for Lord Raglan to have spared such an officer, with a sufficient staff for this service, in the pressing circumstances of his position in the Crimea. The committee, in conclusion, cannot but remark, that the first real improvements in the lamentable condition of the hospitals at Scutari, are to be attributed to private suggestions, private exertions, and private benevolence. Miss Nightingale, at the suggestion of the Secretary-at-War, with admirable devotion, organised a band of nurses and undertook the care of the sick and wounded. A fund, raised by public subscription, was administered by the proprietors of the *Times* newspaper, through Mr. McDonald, an intelligent and, zealous agent. The Hon. and Rev. Sidney Godolphin Osborne, Mr. Augustus Stafford and the Hon. Jocelyn Percy, after a personal inspection of the hospitals, furnished valuable reports and suggestions to government. By these means, much suffering was alleviated, the spirits of the men were raised and many lives saved.

It appears that the sufferings of the army resulted mainly from the circumstances in which the expedition to the Crimea was undertaken and executed. The administration which ordered the expedition had no adequate information as to the amount of force in the Crimea or Sevastopol. They were not acquainted with the strength of the fortresses to be attacked, or with the resources of the country to be invaded. They hoped and expected that the expedition would be immediately successful, and, as they did not foresee the probability of a protracted struggle. They made no provision for a winter campaign; what was planned and undertaken without sufficient information, was conducted without sufficient care or forethought. This conduct on the part of the administration was the first and chief cause of the calamities which befell our army.

End of Volume III

REFERENCES

[1] – private letter to the Duke of Newcastle dated 28th October

[2] – *Hell Riders* by Terry Brighton pg 172

[3] – *ibid*

[4] – *Hell Riders* by Terry Brighton pg 191 if you wish to read the full story of Private John Vahey

[5] – *ibid* pg 197

[6] – *ibid* pg 198 if you wish to read the entire article

[7] – *Hell Riders* by Terry Brighton pg 205

[8] – *A W Kinglake vol V* pg 375

[9] – *A W Kinglake vol VI* pg 42

[10] – *A W Kinglake vol VI* pg 145

[11] – *A W Kinglake vol VI* pg 185

[12] – *A W Kinglake vol VI* pg 235

[13] – *A W Kinglake vol VI* pg 261

[14] – *London Morning Herald* correspondent 8th November

[15] – *A W Kinglake vol VI* pg 264

[16] – *A W Kinglake vol VI* pg 374

[17] – *A W Kinglake vol VI* pg 414

[18] – *A W Kinglake vol VI* pg 431

[19] – *A W Kinglake vol VI* pg 447

[20] – *A W Kinglake vol VI* pg 466 official returns

[21] – *A W Kinglake vol VII* pg 112

[22] – *A W Kinglake vol VII* pg 177

INDEX

Wednesday 25th October 1854; tired, hungry soldiers of Lord Ragan's British expeditionary force awake to a chilly Russian morning only to hear Turkish guns firing down from the Causeway Heights at a massive Russian army advancing upon them and the British port of Balaclava. Five hours later and the British cavalry, under the command of the Earl of Cardigan, careered down the north plain right into the face of the Russian guns and cavalry gathered across the valley. To the astonishment of the Russian army (and no doubt Lord Raglan and his staff) the Light Brigade, despite frightful losses, attacked the guns and fought gallantly against terrible odds before retreating to safety. Had attacked the wrong guns?

'In writing this series I have attempted to update the events of the charge with the aid of modern aerial maps. In doing so, I aim to clear the Earl of Cardigan of any suggestion of blame for the disaster. The blame for the many unjust accusations is, in my opinion, solely the responsibility of Lord Raglan and Lord Lucan, the cavalry commanders.

Stephen Bloom 2017

Clearing Cardigan IV

Lieutenant General James Thomas Brudenell, 7th Earl of Cardigan at the Charge of the Light Brigade 1854

Stephen Bloom

CONTENTS

PREFACE

Generally speaking I should really know of this tragic military event from some distant history lessons about Cardigan and the Charge of the Light Brigade way back in 1854. I also remember a terrible old film in black and white with a dashing Errol Flynn in it, plus a more modern and excellent 1968 version with Cardigan portrayed by Trevor Howard. *"Forward, the Light Brigade! Was there a man dismay'd? Not tho' the soldier knew, someone had blunder'd: theirs not to make reply, theirs not to reason why, theirs but to do and die: into the valley of death rode the six hundred."* – Alfred, Lord Tennyson December 9th 1854. Into the valley of death rode the 600, said the poet laureate. I find that things were actually quite different. For a start it should have been the 700 (673 men by most accounts). The Light Brigade was destroyed? In all about 113 men were killed – or nearly 17% of the force, but even more were wounded – 134 men, or nearly 20% of the brigade. That's 37%, or more than a third of the men killed and wounded. Over 70.5% (about 475) horses were also killed.

Did the brigade attack their Russian enemy at the end of the correct valley, or did Lord Cardigan or Lord Lucan select the wrong one, and why? Cardigan blamed his brother-in-law Lucan for the error. Lucan blamed Raglan, the commander-in-chief for his ambiguous attack order. And what had Captain Nolan to do with it; carrying the message from Raglan to Lucan and then perhaps pointing down the wrong valley – before he could correct the error to Lord Cardigan, Nolan was blown to bits on the battlefield, the first casualty of the charge. Unlike General George Custer's battlefield in Montana, the valley of death has not been preserved to the same extent. Farmer's fields cover the area with what looks like vineyards in places. Where Russian guns and cavalry stood in astonishment at the far end of the valley near a Roman style aqueduct now stands Ukrainian houses (also half way down the valley, too).

The hilly redoubts on the south side of the valley called the Causeway Heights by the British, once held allied cannon manned by Turks until they were seized by Russians in a prelude to Cardigan's charge, are now well eroded with time. But much of it still remains, and with aerial photographs and old maps I hope to show the close location of where battle was fought. To the end of his days and much since then, the 7th Earl of Cardigan, James Thomas Brudenell, was often blamed for the disaster. He was a strict man with his men and no wonder, since as colonel of his regiment (11th Hussars) he had to pay and maintain it mostly at his own expense. That was the way of things back then. In the chapters that follow I shall examine other historian's findings and comments, and particularly the history and newspaper transcripts from 1854.

So the first two volumes of this work will need to be a resume of this war, as I understand it, and the reasons it came about. Thereafter in the third volume I go through Inkerman and in volume IV cover any salient points in my effort to credit Cardigan. In the finale I believe the reader will understand the facts as we know them and must conclude that Cardigan himself was just one of many brave heroes during that bloody day in October 1854; that he certainly was not to blame for what happened and really deserves high recognition to some degree. Also included you will find a vast number of photos of the people involved where available and battle scene location maps, which I think give a nice realism to things; after all, as with General Custer back in 1876, it's nice to put a face to a name, isn't it?

Stephen Bloom, England 2017

PHOTOGRAPHS OF PEOPLE INVOLVED

All photos freely available on the world wide net, unless otherwise stated. Many are of people photographed in later years of their lives: Colonel R Tylden by Roger Fenton; Aimable-Jean-Jacques Pélissier by Fenton; J Estcourt by Fenton.

ILLUSTRATIONS

10. THE END OF THE WAR

War recommences again – Eupatoria

The battle for Sevastopol was not over yet, despite bad winter conditions. On 17th February 1855, the battle for Eupatoria, a once Russian occupied town close to the British and French landing grounds of September 1854, commenced. The Turks had control of the area and were surprisingly vigilant. Upon orders from the Czar himself, who was fearful of a wider Turkish offensive on the Russian flank, a Russian expeditionary force was formed under General Stepan Khrulev which aimed to storm Eupatoria with a force estimated to be between 20,000 to 30,000 men. Khrulev's intentions failed, however, as both the Turk garrison and the Allied fleet offshore anticipated his attack. Russian artillery and infantry attacks were countered by heavy allied artillery fire, and after failing to make any progress after three hours (and with mounting casualties), Khrulev ordered a retreat.

This defeat led to the dismissal of Russian Commander-in-Chief Menshikov; he was replaced by Prince Mikhail Dmitrievich Gorchakov. Tsar Nicholas I also died a week or so after this battle, on 21st February 1855; his son Alexander II took the Russian throne. From a strategic point of view, Eupatoria confirmed that allied total command of the sea could threaten the Russian flank and would continue to do so for the duration of the war. From the allied point of view, possession of Eupatoria meant that a total attack on Sevastopol would now be a viable option. For the Turks, their army had regained some self-esteem and its reputation; the French and British saw this although they would still refuse to make further use of Turkish fighting abilities during the remainder of the Crimean war.

The siege continues

On the allied side of things, the siege of Sevastopol shifted to the right-hand sector of the lines, against the fortifications of the Russian Malakoff. On 22nd March 1855 there was fighting against the French by 5500 Russians over the fort of Mamelon, located on a hill in front (south-east) of the Malakoff fortifications. The French held out and the Russians were forced to retreat back into Sevastopol. On Easter Sunday 8th April 1855, the allies began a heavy bombardment of Sevastopol's defences, employing for the first time the mortar, which fired an exploding projectile in an arc from a position out of sight of the enemy. For the next ten days, the allies silenced the Russian guns along the defence perimeter, but there was no allied infantry assault to complete the mission! On the night of 19th April, Lieutenant Colonel Thomas Graham Egerton attacked the rifle pits before the Redan with his 77th regiment.

The 77th drove out the Russians at the point of the bayonet, not firing a single shot. A detachment of the 77th captured two Russian rifle pits. But towards morning, the enemy made a determined attempt to recover their pits and the men of the 77th charged and drove them away. Captain Lempriere, a very young favourite of Egerton's, was mortally wounded whilst standing next to his colonel. Egerton carried him to a place of shelter; Egerton was then shot through the head and died. His men carried his body back to camp, meeting his wife on the way.

Change of commanders

On 3rd May 1855 the allies sent a British – French naval expedition to capture the eastern Crimean port of Kerch, a sailing distance from Balaclava of about 180 miles. The plan was to then enter the Azov Sea, to undermine Russian communications and supplies arriving for besieged Sevastopol. The force consisted of about 10,000 men, three-quarters of whom were French under the command of General d'Autemarre and Admiral Braut; the British were commanded by George Brown and Admiral Lyons. Everything did not proceed well initially, with General Canrobert receiving conflicting telegrams from Paris regarding a planned attack outside Sevastopol against the Russians in the McKenzie Heights, involving French reserve forces under General Larchey from Constantinople, and the Turkish Army. He intended to recall the French fleet then on its way to Kerch! Lord Raglan was able to signal to Lyons and Brown that they could proceed alone if they so wished, or return; the Russian forces, although superior in number, were spread well out in the area and Kerch itself likely to be within the capability of the British forces to secure alone.

The attack on Kerch

In the event both fleets, British and French, turned about. There had been confusion on dry land between General Canrobert, the French commander-in-chief, and French Emperor Louis Napoleon back home in Paris. The result had been the recall of the allied Kerch flotilla for use bringing up Larchey's reserve forces from Constantinople for a counterstrike against the Russians. Thus the allied commanders held conferences on 12th and 14th May. Raglan, Canrobert and the Turkish commander Omar Pasha, discussed Louis Napoleon's plan for the future conduct of the war. It was agreed that the Turks would move south to Sevastopol from their base at Eupatoria; the French and British would advance upon the McKenzie Heights towards Baktchi Serai (Bakchysaray).

The siege of Sevastopol would be continued by the French and the Turks, according to Buckingham Palace! But this the French and Turks admitted they could not achieve. Canrobert suggested dividing the British troops into two smaller armies. This the British would not do either – the problem was that Paris suggested 30,000 French troops, with an equal number of Turks, but the Turks could only supply half that, and all three commanders thought 90,000 men was the minimum needed to maintain the siege of Sevastopol. France had no real grasp, it appeared, on reality in the field and this, along with the constant tension of command, were some of the reasons why General Canrobert resigned voluntarily on 16th May and handed control of French forces in the Crimea to General Aimable-Jean-Jacques Pélissier.

Offered command by Paris of a Corps, Canrobert declined but continued to serve as French 1st Division's commander; he informed the emperor that part of his reasoning for resigning was the non-cooperation of the English following his recalling of the Kerch mission! General Pelissier was on the task immediately he assumed command of French forces; the move towards McKenzie Heights, thus cutting off completely Sevastopol from reinforcement, was made on 25th May by combined forces of France, England, Turkey and Sardinia. Fifteen-thousand troops arrived from Sardinia under the command of Italian General Alfonso Ferrero Cavaliere La Marmora, and took up position on the French right.

Alfonso Marmora   *Prince Gorchakov*   *Auguste d'Angely*

George Brown lands at Kerch

General Canrobert was involved in Pelissier's action, taking control from the Russians of the Tractir Bridge and the opposite bank of the Tchernaya River as far as the Inkerman Heights and Fedioukine Hills. That allied naval task sent to seize Kerch was also back on. Canrobert's dithering regarding the first mission to Kerch had bought time for the Russian garrison to set up big guns around the town and to sink warships, some containing explosives, in the Kerch Straits. But the allies now had some 5000 Turkish troops to join them on this second expedition, which sailed on 22nd May under command of the same senior officers as before: Lyons, Brown, Bruat and d'Autemarre. This time, the immediate objective at Kerch was seized un-opposed, plus nearby Yeni Kale.

Allied warships destroyed installations and shipping in the Sea of Azov. The Russian commander, Wrengel, however, had already destroyed most Russian guns, government property, over 4,000,000 lbs of corn and 5,000,000 lbs of flour (according to the Russian government), before escaping through the Isthmus to Russia. Thus on the morning of the 25th most of the Kerch region was under allied command and Sir George Brown led the march of his troops through the town and beyond to Yeni Kale. There was much looting (mainly livestock) by the troops, particularly by the Turks (but including some French) who had to be restrained eventually by exacerbated French and British forces.

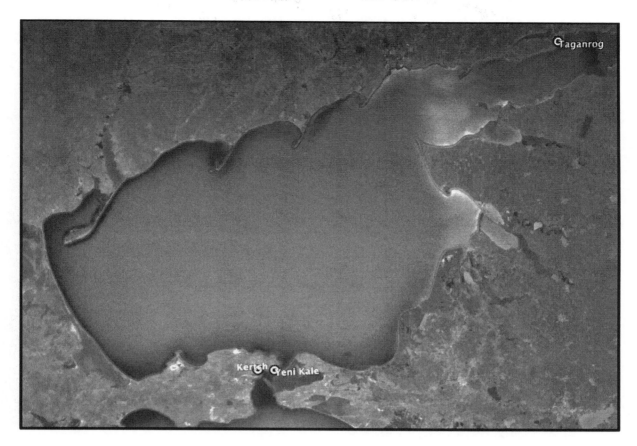

Kerch, Yeni Kale, Taganrog (courtesy Google earth).

Troops were sent by George Brown to Kerch to restore order – not just from joyous troops but also Tartars, who were causing trouble and were the enemy of native Russians, although friends of the allies. Despite these headaches, it seems that a reasonable peace was maintained on land, and the joint allied naval squadrons had much success sinking enemy shipping (about 500 vessels over the next month) and landing troops ashore (Taganrog on the sea of Azov for example). Mostly, the landing parties destroyed food stuffs (corn etc.), government buildings and anything connected with the Russian war effort.

Death at Sevastopol

News of the success from Kerch spread joy amongst the allied troops surrounding Sevastopol. But perhaps few, if any, of the allied men were aware that there had already been peace negotiations (in Vienna) with a view to ending the war; these had broken down in the end but could have succeeded if only the successes of Kerch had occurred earlier, when Canrobert had ordered the return of the French fleet. Nevertheless, the armies laying siege to Sevastopol prepared for another attempt to take the town. Prior to this, and lasting several months, a cholera epidemic spread rapidly among the Sardinian troops and the number of deaths quadrupled suddenly. Italian General Marmora fell ill on 4th June and died on the night of the 6th at Kadikoi; so rapidly had the sickness spread.

3rd Bombardment

Allied guns commenced firing again at Sevastopol in the afternoon of 6th June, continuing on the following day though to no avail. The time was ripe for charging and seizing the Russian redoubts surrounding the town. For this, Lord Raglan had concurred with General Pelissier and provision made, albeit in small quantity, for such an attack. This followed what was called the third bombardment (of 1855) on 6th and 7th June, when at dawn the French advanced on the Mamelon 'Lunette' Bastion in an attempt to take the Malakov. There were some gains made, such as the two small 'White Redoubts' to the northeast of the town (the Selinghinksk and Volhynia), but formidable fortifications of the Redan still lay unconquered.

The Mamelon fell, but the French had been disrupted by a dispute between Pelissier and Bosquet, the corps commander, which led to General Auguste Michel Étienne Regnaud de Saint-Jean d'Angély taking over Bosquet's corps, on the eve of the renewed assault on Russian defences. The British were likewise involved on the left flank of the French as they stormed Mamelon and advanced towards the base of the Malakoff, from where they were forced to retreat to the seized Mamelon again.

The British attack was towards the Great Redan, in front of which stood an area called the Quarries that were to be taken under the supervision of the senior commander there, Colonel Horatio Shirley. Two British wings attacked the Quarries, under Colonel Robert Campbell and Major James Armstrong. Campbell was wounded twice, but continued to lead his men; likewise, Armstrong, who was disabled but refused to be moved to safety. Despite a heavy enemy fire from the Redan, British engineers under Colonel Richard Tylden managed to extend during the night the seized Russian trenches of the Quarries, with the foremost trenches on the British side. At daybreak, the Russians counter attacked the British in the trenches, who had hardly the strength to resist but did. This victory cost more than 5000 men killed and wounded: the French 5443 and the British 672. And all to advance a little closer to Sevastopol!

Sevastopol defences June 1855

4th Bombardment

The bombardment by the allies of Sevastopol continued for a further three days, after which a so called fourth bombardment was scheduled for 17th June against the Redan, or Greater Redan as it was often called. This was to begin with seaborne attack from the combined French and British fleets, with land bombardment from the combined artillery strength. But as was common with French military leadership at the time, their commanding officer, Pelissier, changed the plan at the last moment without informing Lord Raglan! This was to dispense with the preliminary dawn bombardment, and instead for the troops to attack piecemeal. Raglan only learned of it after returning to his headquarters, and only then from his chief engineer! Raglan and the British therefore conformed to Pelissier's new plan; so at dawn the allied attack force was in position, following a night of allied bombardment of Sevastopol.

Charles Windham

William Massy

Napoléon Bonaparte

Lacy Yea*

Gerald Graham

* Courtesy HM Queen Elizabeth II royal collection/Fenton

The Storm

The attack was by no less than three French divisions, under General's Mayran, Brunet and d'Autemarre; their mission – to take the Malakoff. On the east side near the Little Redan, the French advanced at the wrong time, due to a mistake in signals, and so found the going difficult; their general, Mayran, was killed. On the centre, Brunet's men were dithering because they had not mistaken the go signal, and despite Pelissier ordering General de Saint-Jean d'Angély to support Mayran with the French Guards, the forces appeared to be not moving. When Brunet finally moved, he was killed too – his men were stopped short at about a hundred yards or so of the Little Redan. Some of d'Autemarre's men managed to break through via a ravine and turn on the Malakoff from within Russian defences.

The French held the ground, but were now under attack from two flanks: from the Malakoff and the Great Redan, which halted their advance. To assist the French, Lord Raglan decided to commit his troops in two flanks against the Great Redan: on the west side commanded by General John Campbell, and on the east Brigadier (Colonel) Lacy Walter Giles Yea. Campbell's men came mainly from 4th Division, 57th regiment in particular, and was to be the 'storming' party equipped with ladders, numbering about 682 men.

There was a reserve of about 800 men drawn from the 21st Fusiliers and 17th regiment commanded by Colonel Lord West – General Campbell went to the front of his men to conduct the assault. There was a distance of nearly 500 yards to traverse to the Redan, and this would expose the British, no thanks to Pelissier's decision to attack early instead of following heavy bombardment prior to the off, to intense Russian fire. Lieutenant Murray, the officer commanding the engineers accompanying Campbell, was killed; command now fell upon the head of the 'ladder' party, young Lieutenant Gerald Graham.

During the halt, Colonel Richard Tylden appeared to encourage the engineers forward; he was struck down and seriously wounded, dying some months later. As the British advanced against the enemy, General John Campbell was shot dead, along with Colonel Shadforth, commander of 57th regiment; Colonel Lord West took command from Campbell and Colonel Warre from Shadforth. Warre needed reinforcements but none were available, and he could not proceed farther. The ladder party under Lieutenant Graham tried again to reach the Redan but could not; Lord West sent a message to General George Brown, who was in overall command of the attack on the Redan and commander of the Light Division. Brown told the messenger that there was no reply to West's last request! And so ended the left flank attack on the Redan.

Richard Tylden

Aimable Pélissier

Harry Jones

The cost in lives was 177 men killed and wounded, along with 15 officers and one general. Directly in front of Lord Raglan's position was the south tip of Sevastopol Harbour, with Russian artillery called the 'Peressip Battery' facing the British trenches. Behind these was rising ground where Lord Raglan watched events. There was one noticeable success here; General William Eyre led 1st brigade (2000 men) from 3rd Division (Richard England), and made an early start before attempting, successfully, to bridge the Peressip area.

Eyre continued to hold his gains all day, but failures elsewhere made this impracticable except for a few useful buildings that British engineers felt worthy of the risk. The loss in men and officers killed and wounded, was a massive 562! Colonel Yea, acting brigadier general, had 692 men plus 800 in his reserve force for his eastern flank; they were likely to be attacked by not only the Redan defenders, but those from the Malakoff on their right. The ladder party and engineers were able to advance very close to the Redan, within 80 yards, but the fire from the Russians was intense. Lieutenant A'Court Fisher, leading the engineers with Lieutenant Graves leading the ladder party, saw Colonel Yea approaching their location and asked him whether the engineers should advance in preparation for the advancing columns.

Yea had no time to reply, as he was shot dead by the enemy. A'Court Fisher had only 150 men in his location, and no officer senior than himself. In true military tradition, by deciding they could not secure the Redan, he ordered a retreat back to the trenches. Everything told, the British east flank lost 313 men killed or wounded. During all this mayhem and death, Lord Raglan and his staff remained on high ground, called the 3rd parallel, some 600 yards south of the end of the harbour at Sevastopol, and equidistant between the Flagstaff and Great Redan. His view must have been spectacular of the proceedings.

General Harry Jones, the chief engineer who was there, was shot in the forehead but survived. Other men, bringing messages, were not so lucky if they did not keep low. Lord Raglan decided to let loose his artillery against the Redan before riding across the 1.8 miles to find General Pelissier to confer. Things were no better on the French side; yes, they held some parts of the Malakoff but needed reinforcement – in ordering forward reserves, the French lost their gains to the Russians because French reserves were too far back and took too long to get into position. And so both sides withdrew, with large losses and still no major gains.

James Estcourt *Frank Burghersh* *St Michael & All Angels*

Death of Lord Raglan

Cholera was still prevalent in the allied camps after the fourth bombardment concluded. Several officers visiting British HQ noticed the change of appearance in the commander-in-chief; he was more stricken when his adjutant general, James Estcourt, succumbed on 24th June to disease. The day before, Lord Raglan became unwell, although he was still able to function with his dispatches to home; he still inspected the troops and the field hospitals treating the wounded. On the 25th he was much grief stricken but still attended the burial plot of his friend, James Estcourt, who had just been buried. By the 26th Lord Raglan felt feint and his doctor, Prendergast, recommended bed rest. The following day, Raglan sent a telegram home announcing that he was sick. He was no worse (or better for that matter) the following day. In the afternoon of the 28th Raglan's servant called Dr Prendergast to announce that his lordship had deteriorated, and by 4:30 p.m. the doctor could see that Lord Raglan was sinking quickly.

General Airey was at Raglan's side and asked repeatedly if he would like to see anyone; the chief said no, until finally asking to see Lord Frank Burghersh, his wife's nephew (actually

Colonel Francis William Henry Fane, 12th Earl of Westmorland). The army head of the church, Archdeacon Wright, gave the last rites after sunset, immediately upon which the allied commander-in-chief died. Also present at the end, besides Airey, Burghersh and Archdeacon Wright, were Colonel Somerset, Dr Prendergast, Lady Agnes Charlotte Paget and Colonel Thomas Steele.

The following day, various senior officers from all the allied forces came to HQ to pay their respects. General Canrobert was there, as was General Pelissier, who was reported to have wept for about an hour. That same day, the news was broken to the men by General James Simpson's morning general order, as well as to Queen Victoria. A general order dated 4th July 1855 from army commander-in-chief (Lord Hardinge) expressed her majesty's deep regret at the loss of Lord Raglan, and her wish that her sentiments be communicated to the army; she wrote personally to Lady Raglan with her condolences.

Back in the Crimea, on 3rd July, the roads between British HQ and the French Port of Kazatch were lined with troops as the funeral cortege moved the coffin on a cannon, draped in the union flag and with Lord Raglan's feathery hat and sword placed upon. Behind it rode the current commanders of the allied forces, followed by Lord Raglan's favourite horse, saddled, riderless and led by orderlies. Following the death procession, came officers from all branches of the military: army, navy, marines. The Russians that day remained silent as the remains of Lord Raglan were placed on the navy ship *Caradoc* for repatriation to England and then burial at the family church of St Michael & All Angels in Great Badminton, Gloucester.

The end for Sevastopol

The new, short term and very reluctant commander-in-chief in Lord Raglan's place was General James Simpson. On 5th September 1855, the French commenced a sixth bombardment of Sevastopol, followed on 8th September by a successful attack and capture of the Malakoff Bastion. The Little Redan did not fall, and neither did the British capture the Great Redan. The French army was under the command of General Marie Esme Patrice Maurice de MacMahon, and they successfully stormed Malakoff Bastion whereas a simultaneous British attack on the Redan failed. The French under Bosquet raised the tricolour flag on top of this stubborn Russian redoubt. The French also took to hand fighting with the Russians along the Flagstaff and Central Bastions; by the following day, the allies entered triumphantly the burning remains of Sevastopol, only to find that the Russians had evacuated the place and fled to the high ground around the McKenzie Farm! British General James Simpson resigned as commander-in-chief on the 10th November 1855 and was replaced the next day by General William John Codrington.

Marie de MacMahon

War ends

The end of the Crimean war began with peace negotiations at the Congress of Paris, and finally resulted in the signing of the Treaty of Paris on 30th March 1856. Russia restored to the Turks the city of Kars, and all other parts of the Turkish territory of which the Russian troops were in possession. Britain, France, Sardinia and Turkey restored to Russia the towns and ports of Sevastopol, Balaklava, Kamish, Eupatoria, Kerch, Jeni kale, Kinburn, as well as all other territories occupied by the allied troops. The Tsar and the Sultan agreed not to establish naval or military arsenals on the Black Sea coast; these Black Sea clauses weakened Russia, and so it no longer posed a naval threat to Turkey. Thus the end result was that the British, French, Sardinians and Turks packed up and went home again, after so much bloodshed, from the 12th July 1856.

11. SUMMARY NEXT

It has been a long journey for us from the allied landings at Calamita Bay, so we should refresh ourselves briefly as to what happened in the lead up to the charge of the Light Brigade. The allied landings began from 14th September 1854 at Calamita, a distance of around 38 miles' march following the coast to the Star Fort north Sevastopol. On the way, the battle of the Alma was fought and the allied coalition tested for the first time. Until then, we had seen that the British were quite disorganized in their preparation compared to the French, but in actual battle the British were bold and the French slow to attack.

Lord Lucan's cavalry, or only half of it since Scarlett's Heavy Brigade had not landed yet, was used only in a brief reconnaissance role – Lord Cardigan rather foolishly (because he did not know how many enemy he was facing) demanded of Lucan a charge, which Lucan sensibly refused. After the Alma, French commander St Arnaud was slow to move on towards the next target, Sevastopol, since his men needed to retrieve their packs and rest, apparently.

French reconnaissance had also informed him of the Russian Star Fort construction and other fortifications north of the port that he would shortly run into, and he did not want to attack right away. The result of this dithering was that the allies next moved off at an oblique angle of around 20° from the required direction, to pass Sevastopol to the east, instead of via a direct attack track and worse still, allowing a majority of enemy soldiers at the port to escape to the northeast.

The enemy tail was intercepted by the British near Mackenzie's Farm, and a number of goods wagons taken as booty. But the Light Brigade arrived too late to play any part in the British attack. The French occupied the ports of Kamiesh and Kazatch, southwest of Sevastopol, whereas the British occupied the far too small port of Balaclava. On the afternoon of 29th September, French Marshal St. Arnaud died aboard the ship Berthollet from Cholera.

He was replaced by General Canrobert. Meanwhile, the Russian garrison at Sevastopol built defence works under the supervision of Colonel Franz Todleben. Lord Raglan committed all four of his army divisions to the upcoming siege duties. There were also a number of hastily built redoubts situated along Woronzoff Road, and these were protected and operated by Turks, with British advisors helping.

Outside Kadikoi village, just one battalion of the 93rd Sutherland Highlanders kept watch on the port, with some Royal Marines under Colonel Hurdle northeast of Balaclava on higher ground. The eventual siege bombardment started on 17th October. The effects of this bombardment on the Russian garrison was negligible, and the French appear to have made up their own timetable, instead of sticking to the joint allied plan.

Bombardment from the sea caused damage, but the Russian forts returned damage to many allied ships. Over the coming days, the French rested their guns whilst the British discovered that whatever damage they caused to Russian defences, the following day they had been repaired completely. On 18th October a Russian field army was seen operating within British view on the ridges surrounding the town of Chorgun (or Tchorgoun); this army consisted of horse, foot and artillery pieces, and was about five miles' northeast of Balaclava.

The British army, with their naval artillery, had more or less full control of the Balaklava plains should Menshikov try to attack – 26 guns stood on the hills commanding the defence. The man in charge of all this was Sir Colin Campbell, with six companies of Ainslie's 93rd Sutherland Highlanders Regiment camped just north of Kadikoi. Colonel Hurdle and 1200 Marines controlled the northeast hills and a few guns. A battalion of Turks with field-artillery completed the Balaclava and Kadikoi defences – the British line of defence, the six Redoubts, stretched for about 2.7 miles redoubt to redoubt.

At about three miles from Redoubt 1 lay the village of Chorgun (or Tchorgoun), where Russian commander Pavel Liprandi had based his HQ and stationed his troops. He planned to take the British redoubts and Balaclava with four columns of infantry. General Ryzhov had command of a cavalry brigade (3000 sabres) with two horse artillery batteries of 16 guns. The Russian southern column was led by General Gribbe, with the intention of seizing the village of Kamara to protect Liprandi's left flank.

The centre column was divided in two, with the left centre column commanded by General Semiakin and the right centre column commanded by General Levutski (or Levontski). The centre of the advance would be an assault on Redoubt's 1 and 2. A north column protecting Liprandi's right flank was commanded by Colonel Skiuderi (or Scuderi), and would advance from Tractir to Redoubt 3.

The British redoubts were manned by 1500, possibly unreliable Turks, guided by British officers, with only nine artillery guns between them, and despite time to build up defences, Redoubts 5 & 6 were still not complete. The not inconsiderable Russian force, numbering about 24,000 men, could surely destroy the British and Turkish forces manning the redoubts, and those on the Marine Heights overlooking Balaclava?

The primary assault plan called for seizing a defence line formed by 93rd Sutherland Highlanders, and a Turkish camp established near the village of Kadikoi. From these locations the bombardment and seizure of the Port of Balaclava could commence. The Russian cavalry and their artillery guns would enter the east end of the north valley and await further orders from General Liprandi. During all this, reserve forces under General Zhaboritski were to leave the area of Mackenzie's Farm and descend to the edge of the Fedioukine Heights, setting up their guns above the north valley.

Despite advanced warning of the impending attack from Turkish spies, Lord Raglan issued no further orders! This was likely due to an erroneous report of a similar nature of 21st October that resulted in 1000 men from 4th Division marching from Sapoune Heights only to be sent back again when it was deemed the enemy had not advanced. Lord Raglan obviously felt that such information from spies had to be viewed as unreliable. So, as was the practice in 1854, the cavalry turned out for inspection an hour before dawn on the morning of Wednesday 25th October 1854.

Lord Lucan inspected them before riding off at a walk towards Redoubt 1, Canrobert's Hill, with his staff. Lord Cardigan was still asleep in his yacht in Balaclava harbour; dawn began to break the eastern horizon as Lucan, Paulet, McMahon and Paget approached that crucial redoubt. It was light enough for the party to notice that two flag ensigns were flying from the flag pole. The staff party were at first confused as to what the signals meant, and discussed it freely. One of them thought it was the signal that the enemy was advancing. Still others doubted it until the redoubt suddenly opened fire with her 12 pound guns.

Lord George Paget rode at speed to the camp of the Light Brigade. He was colonel in command of 4th Light Dragoons and was next senior officer in the Light Brigade to Lord Cardigan; in his chief's absence, Paget mounted up the brigade. Lord Lucan and Colin Campbell, from the Causeway Heights, saw the enemy advancing from the direction of Chorgun and Baider Heights. Lucan sent an aide-de-camp, Captain Charteris, to army HQ to alert them of impending attack.

Lucan also ordered the heavy cavalry forward, along with Captain Maude's horse artillery troop guns. Maude stopped his guns on the right hand side of Redoubt 3. The Light Brigade remained on the southern slopes of the Causeway Heights close to Redoubt 6, and Lucan, with Colin Campbell's approval, rode out with Scarlett's Heavy Brigade to show a threatening force to the enemy. The maneuvering of the brigade made no difference to the Russians, for they continued to advance; I believe a more experienced commander than Lord Lucan might well have checked the advancing enemy without any loss of the regiments involved.

For there were men with overseas cavalry experience in India or Spain, who did exist and were serving or leading regiments – but Lucan did not call upon their experience that morning. The Russians continued and Major General Gribbe, with just three battalions, took possession of Kamara and set up his guns facing Redoubt 1 at a range of about 1500 yards. From Chorgun came the battalions of Generals Semiakin and Levutski, who bore down upon Redoubts 1 and 2. Also moving down at the same time from Tractir was Colonel Scuderi and his men, whilst Russian cavalry and all their 30 artillery guns entered the north valley at the far end and made ready to support the advancing troops.

Allied Redoubts 1 to 3 responded, until Captain Maude was seriously injured and Lucan ordered them to withdraw; the Turks manning the redoubts also fled towards Balaclava. The redoubts fell, with the remaining guns spiked by British soldiers before they too fled with the Turks; many of them joined the right-hand side of 93rd Sutherland Highlanders at Kadikoi. Nevertheless, the first three redoubts fell to the Russians. Next we come to Lord Raglan's first orders of the day; from his vantage point on Sapoune Heights he decided to reinforce Lucan and Campbell and made the decision to send two infantry divisions down from Sevastopol to defend Balaclava: 1st Division under Cambridge and 4th Division under Cathcart.

Cambridge was to descend from the heights into the south valley, whilst Cathcart, stationed further south, was to assist Colin Campbell and 93rd Sutherland Highlanders at Balaclava. Historians have often said that the order to Cathcart was ambiguous in detail, but that the staff officer entrusted with the order was in no doubt as to its meaning. This officer (unnamed) was met by General Airey who told him, under no circumstances was he to direct 4th Division via Woronzoff Road (the Causeway Heights, probably because the redoubts at the far end had been seized by the enemy and also British cavalry were stationed at the western end of them).

With this and Raglan's message, he rode fast to 4th Division HQ to find Cathcart in his tent; the gist of the conversation is that the officer told Sir George that Lord Raglan requests he move his division immediately to the assistance of the Turks, and that the divisional commander said that it was quite impossible for 4th Division to move. The startled staff officer replied that his orders were very positive and that the Russians were advancing upon Balaclava. Cathcart replied that he couldn't help that; that the greater portion of his men had only just come in from night duty in the trenches – and then he invited the officer to join him for breakfast!

The officer politely declined dining with Cathcart and reiterated his orders once more from Lord Raglan – this time, crucially changing assistance of the Turks to assistance of Colin Campbell. Sir Colin had just the 93rd with him, he said, and the Turks were in full flight from the redoubts. Cathcart replied that if the officer would not sit down in his tent, then he may as well go back to Lord Raglan and tell him 4th Division could not move! The staff officer saluted and left, but quickly returned to Cathcart, pointing out that he had orders to remain until the division was ready to move out.

After respectfully arguing his point, Sir George finally said very well, that he would consult with his own staff officers as to whether anything could be done. He went away and a short time later, the division marched away towards The Col. Lord Raglan was suspicious that the Balaclava attack might be just a feint to enable the Russians at Sevastopol to attack the weakened allied forces there, so accordingly he sent another ADC, Lieutenant Calthorpe, to appraise Richard England (3rd Division) of the evolving situation.

As the attack unfolded, French commander-in-chief Canrobert rode up on to the Sapoune Heights to survey the situation for himself. After much dithering he sent two brigades to wait at the foot of the heights. This included General Viscount Armand-Octave-Marie d'Allonville with 1st Regiment de Chasseurs d'Afrique, and 4th Regiment de Chasseurs d'Afrique: 1500 sabres in all.

Near Kadikoi gorge, Lord Lucan was waiting for his own orders from Lord Raglan; eventually they arrived and disappointingly, the cavalry was not to become entangled in combat until the arrival of the two divisions in support of the Turks and Colin Campbell. Lord Raglan sent Captain Wetherall down with further orders; the order was for the cavalry division to withdraw to the left of Redoubt 6 and the foothills of the Sapoune Heights.

'Cavalry to take ground to the left of second line of redoubts occupied by Turks.' What is this 'second line of redoubts'? The Turks had fled by this time, leaving only Redoubts 4, 5 and 6 in British hands – Redoubt 4 was unfinished and thus unoccupied. So, at Lord Lucan's request, Captain Wetherall waited to see that the order was implemented in accordance with Lord Raglan's meaning. Wetherall knew Raglan's request, even if the written order made little sense!

When completed satisfactorily, the main part of the allied effort to defend Balaclava now stood at the western end of the plains. In doing this, we see the thought processes of Lord Lucan; like me, he thought Lord Raglan's order ambiguous. So as not to endanger the cavalry division and be made a scape goat, he preferred additional confirmation of Raglan's requirement – under battle conditions, however, this would hardly be practicable, and he would have to think and interpret orders on his own.

The distance from the cavalry division to Colin Campbell's 93rd Sutherland Highlanders was now about 1⅓ miles, but from a technical view point Sir Colin was not supported. Nothing could be done until Cambridge and Cathcart put in an appearance on the likely battlefield. Liprandi, in observing the route to Balaclava, would have seen the only thing barring the Russians was Colin Campbell and 400 men of 93rd Sutherland Highlanders under their colonel, William Bernard Ainslie, plus 100 invalid men under Colonel Daveney and a battery gun detachment; also two battalions of Turks. Liprandi did not act immediately, however.

The Sutherland Highlanders were quickly reinforced by the arrival of Major Gordon with two further battalions, who had been supporting the Marines and Turks on the Marine Heights; they now numbered 550 men. The location was the rising ground in front of the village of Kadikoi, with its attendant gorge and the road to The Col and Sevastopol – also known as Dunrobin, or Sutherland Hillock. At around 8:30 the Russians placed artillery just within range of Sir Colin's men and opened fire, injuring a couple of soldiers and some Turks; Sir Colin immediately withdrew the line to the foot of the Dunrobin Hillock, where he had them lie down for protection.

In the unlikely event of the Russians breaking through Kadikoi gorge and on to Balaclava, Sir Colin sent Colonel Anthony Sterling back to the harbour to warn the fleet moored there of the impending attack. Russian cavalry was seen moving slowly along the north valley towards Redoubts 3 and 4. Part of it peeled off to the left to pass over the Causeway Heights at Redoubt 3, headed directly towards Kadikoi and the 93rd Sutherland Highlanders.

The British estimated 400 enemy horsemen, whereas Russian engineer Todleben claimed double that number. The Russian cavalry came to within 1000 yards of Dunrobin Hillock before Campbell ordered his troops to stand up. Instead of forming the normal square for repelling cavalry, the 93rd formed a long line, two men deep. Turkish troops on the edges failed to follow this but instead fell back before heading towards Balaclava.

'Remember there is no retreat from here, men!' Campbell shouted. 'You must die where you stand!'

'Ay ay, Sir Colin;' came a reply, 'if needs be we'll do that.'

The men stood on the hillock and assumed their position for fighting in two lines; the attacking Russian squadrons of horse must have been surprised that the red dressed enemy had the gall to stand right before them. They seemed to be preparing to bayonet charge the cavalry and indeed, some might have charged up the hill had not Campbell astride his horse cried out to them.

'Ninety-third, ninety-third; damn all that eagerness!'

They held their ground against all odds, firing their weapons three times and injured a few Russians, but none were seen to fall from their chargers. The enemy turned around and finally wheeled away to the left and their commander, fearing this was a diversion for much bigger allied forces waiting near Kadikoi, headed back the way he had come towards Redoubt 3. Thus we have the battle of the 'thin red line.' The remainder of the Russian cavalry that had not attacked the 93rd continued along towards Redoubt 5, where it halted after receiving just a few shots from the batteries on the far western side of the north valley.

These were possibly from Cambridge's 1st Division, who were in direct line of sight. The Russians then turned left and headed towards Woronzoff Road, where it crossed the Causeway Heights and entered the south valley. The die was now set for the charge of the Heavy Brigade. As the Turks started to withdraw from the thin red line position, Lord Raglan ordered eight squadrons of heavy dragoons move down to support Campbell. This order was sent via the usual channel; through Lord Lucan for Brigadier Scarlett and his Heavy Brigade.

James Scarlett now led the move from the Redoubt 6 position, south-eastwards into the south valley towards Colin Campbell's position. Unknown to Scarlett, Ryzhov's cavalry was waiting static on the south slopes of the Causeway Heights just 800 yards from the Heavy Brigade moving slowly towards Kadikoi. Manoeuvring around a vineyard took time and when clear, it was not immediately apparent that the enemy were watching from a short distance away at Redoubt 5. Cardigan's Light Brigade remained static, unaware because of intervening hills that the Russians had crossed the Causeway Heights just 1000 yards away.

Scarlett led his brigade with his squadrons following in two columns. They cleared the vineyard plantation and then worked through the remaining tents of the Light Brigade camp situated midway between Redoubt 6 and the 93rd Sutherland Highlanders. Scarlett's aide-de-camp, Lieutenant Alexander Elliot, happened to glance to his left to the top of the Causeway Heights, and there saw the tops of cavalry lances. A few moments later and squadrons of Russian cavalry came into view. Scarlett, who was short sighted, took a few moments to see what Elliot had just seen. Scarlett had no scruples about his duty now that the enemy had put in an appearance.

'Are you right in front?' he called across.

'Ay sir!' was the reply.

'Left wheel into line,' was the next order.

The plan was to turn all six heavy squadrons and face the enemy in the charge – some of the brigade were marching left in front, which did not allow for the full operation that Scarlett wanted, so as the left wing turned it formed a line of the Heavy Brigade numbering just 300 sabres. The rest of the brigade were coming up behind. There was no time to issue further orders to get the brigade into one long line, before things became an unstoppable flow. Scarlett led the attack in person; his divisional commander, Lucan and staff, came rushing up from the rear.

Lucan decided that this was an emergency he had to deal with in person without consulting the brigade commander, and ordered the disorganized rear troops to wheel into line, so repeating Scarlett's order to take ground to the right before they could wheel into line. Not all obeyed Lucan's command; fortunately, there seemed no confusion on the pending battlefield and up ahead Scarlett gave the second order for the troops to wheel into line, now having enough width for his squadrons to form up side by side. Scarlett explained rapidly his reasons for taking ground further to the right to Lucan, who had just joined him and received an assurance that the brigade would be supported; thereafter, Lucan issued a direct order to Scarlett:

'General Scarlett; take these four squadrons and at once attack the column of the enemy.'

Lord Lucan was mistaken as to the number of squadrons present and ready – there were not four but just three at that time; but the charge had been sanctioned by him to the relief of General Scarlett and his immediate staff. The scene was now set for the charge. The front row consisting of 300 sabres set off; the second row following a similar number of heavies and the Russian cavalry perched on the Causeway Heights were believed to number 3000 sabres.

A bugle sounded near Redoubt 5 and the mass of Russian cavalry descended towards the British. General Scarlett remained confidently cool as his regiments dressed and redressed in calm preparation; seeing this, the Russians started to falter in their approach. With bugles sounding, their cavalry slowed and then halted! This was too good an opportunity to miss and Lord Lucan ordered the charge sounded by bugle. The Heavy Brigade was too busy preparing to take any immediate notice of the divisional bugle. With the enemy stalled on the slopes of the Causeway Heights, Scarlett turned in the saddle to his bugler.

'Sound the charge,' he said.

Before the bugler had finished blowing the notes, the brigade commander was off at a trot! The gap between him and his regiments was increasing and only intervention from Lieutenant Elliot slowed Scarlett's pace. Turning in the saddle and waving his sword, he shouted 'come on!' to the following troops. With the rest of the brigade lumbering up the steep incline, Scarlett travelled at speed with his aide Lieutenant Elliot, his bugler and an orderly just behind. The Russians gave way and allowed the brigade commander to run through the centre ranks.

The fight was on, with every man having to attack overwhelming numbers of enemy cavalry, but despite the melee the 300 were not in immediate danger of destruction. The mass of Russians finally began to slacken before breaking; they retreated back over the Causeway Heights. Emerging from all this chaos came General Scarlett, with Lord Lucan riding up to him. The brigade, quite rightly from exhaustion, did not pursue the Russian cavalry into the north valley, because of the danger of Russian guns now stationed upon Fedioukine Heights.

The charge (or trot) of the Heavy Brigade lasted between eight to ten minutes; the casualty list cannot be exact and varies – often lists include dead and wounded as one figure. The British appeared to have lost ten killed and up to 98 wounded. Russian casualties were much higher, believed to be about fifty dead and 200 men wounded. A bluntness of sabres, swords and the thickness of Russian great-coats prevented casualties from being so much higher. One result of the charge was that the Russians were more willing to give ground if British cavalry approached their positions again. As the Russians retreated in disarray to the far eastern end of the north valley, cheers were heard from the watching 93rd Sutherland Highlanders on their thin red line, who had a spectacular view of proceedings.

12. SUMMARY OF THE CHARGE

Before we consider those explanations given by Lords Lucan and Cardigan as to the Light Brigade disaster that was shortly to follow the success of the heavies, we should resume as a reminder the sequence of events associated with the demise of both lordships. First, many people believe that to complete victory it would have been proper for the victors to chase and finish off the enemy, if possible. This was not done as you can imagine because the Heavy Brigade was exhausted by their efforts and because British artillery began firing down the north valley. It was also seen that the Russians had placed guns upon the Fedioukine Heights capable of hitting any part of the north valley. But there was a force, of course, nearby that could have chased and harassed the enemy, for at least part of the way along the north valley.

This was the Light Brigade. Standing about 1400 yards from the battle, it remained across the west end of the north valley and did not move. They were mere spectators whilst Scarlett and his men fought for glory on the slopes of the Causeway Heights. Witnesses confirmed the disappointment of Lord Cardigan as his brigade remained stationary. He rode up and down the ranks, muttering to himself repeatedly 'damn those heavies; they have the laugh of us this day!'

Other witnesses in other locations appeared vexed and curious as to why the other half of the British cavalry division had not moved in support of their outnumbered colleagues. The reasons for it is confusing and open to interpretation. Before riding off after the Heavy Brigade, Lord Lucan had been in conversation with his brother-in-law Cardigan, who had been left in the position he occupied with orders to defend it against any Russian attack. Lucan's caveat led Cardigan to conclude that it was his duty to not attack the enemy in flank whilst the Heavy Brigade was attacking in front, and also not attack Russians in retreat.

Lucan did not consider these his parting orders to Cardigan, however. Cardigan's recollection of events, which we shall examine more soon, was as follows: he had been ordered into a particular position by Lucan, his superior officer, with orders on no account to leave it and to defend it against any Russian attack. The enemy did not approach his position, however. Lucan's recollection of events was as follows: he told Cardigan he was going to leave him and that he (Cardigan) should remember that he had been put in that position by Lord Raglan for the defence of it.

Lucan's orders to Cardigan were thus that he was to attack anything and everything that shall come within his reach, but to be careful of columns or squares. However, since no enemy column (cavalry) or squares (infantry) came within reach (they were about 1000 yards away) Cardigan remained static. Not so the commander of 17th Lancers, Captain William Morris; he realized the opportunity and swears he approached Lord Cardigan and pleaded that the opportunity was too good to miss, and that the commander of the Light Brigade refused to move.

Lord Cardigan, in an affidavit, says that Captain Morris never gave him any advice or made any proposal of the sort; it was not his duty to do so and that he did not commit any such irregularity. However, Somerset Calthorpe, an aide to Lord Raglan who was present, confirms Morris' statement. According to James Wightman, also present, Morris pleaded with Cardigan:

'My lord, are you not going to charge the flying enemy?'

'No,' Cardigan replied, 'we have orders to remain here.'

'But my lord, it is our positive duty to follow up this advantage.'

'No, we must remain here.'

'Do, my lord, do allow me to charge them with the 17th. Sir, my lord, they are in disorder.'

'No no, sir,' Cardigan concluded, 'we must not stir from here.'

Lord Lucan, as we might well imagine, was vexed by the failure of Cardigan to act, and sent an aide to him who enjoined him in future to lose no opportunity of making a flank attack. But the horse had bolted, literally! Things might have been easier for the Heavy Brigade had Cambridge and Cathcart arrived in time; the duke was more or less in place where Lord Raglan wanted him to be, but Cathcart was taking much too long to get near the south valley. The delay in the arrival of Cathcart's 4th Division required messengers to speed things along, but they too failed. General Airey was sent to do the business, and in the region of The Col he found Cathcart and spoke to him:

'Sir George Cathcart,' he said, 'Lord Raglan wishes you to advance immediately and recapture the redoubts.'

He then turned to one of Raglan's staff officers, who was present, and said 'you are acquainted with the position of each redoubt; remain with Sir George Cathcart and show him where they are.'

Slowly, the tired 4th Division continued on to the open south plain, moving east and passing empty Redoubts 6 and 5, where Cathcart left some men before marching to Redoubt 4. Here he had his men lay down before ordering the accompanying artillery to open fire on Redoubt 3, then occupied by Russian troops. Lord Raglan was once more vexed by the behaviour of Cathcart and realized that time was running out for a successful conclusion. He therefore decided that the cavalry would be better suited to the task in hand and accordingly sent an order to Lord Lucan on the plain below. This is known as Raglan's 3rd order of that morning, timed at 10:00 a.m. and it read:

'Cavalry to advance and take advantage of any opportunity to recover the heights. They will be supported by the infantry which have been ordered. Advance on two fronts.'

It is difficult to think that such an order could be misconstrued by Lucan, but he did construe it differently from its intention. First, he moved the Light Brigade across the width of the north valley, before moving the tired Heavy Brigade on to the slopes of Causeway Heights near Redoubt 6, there to await arrival of the promised infantry which had still not arrived. The cavalry then remained at the halt for about fifty-five minutes! The plan appeared now that infantry would take the heights with the cavalry in support. Lord Raglan and his staff, meanwhile, watched from above on Sapoune Heights and saw the cavalry remain at the halt.

Using field glasses, it was seen that the Russians had brought forward teams of horses with lasso tackle attached, and that they probably intended to remove the British guns left on the eastern redoubts. Lord Raglan now turned to General Airey and told him to copy down a new order for Lord Lucan. At 10:45 a.m. the infamous 4th order of the morning was written out by Airey as Raglan dictated. It read:

'Lord Raglan wishes the cavalry to advance rapidly to the front – follow the enemy and try to prevent the enemy carrying away the guns – troop horse artillery may accompany – French cavalry is on your left (signed R Airey) immediate.'

Fate played its hand as misunderstanding after misunderstanding beckoned disaster. Lord Raglan's aide, Lieutenant Calthorpe, was back on hand to deliver this urgent new order, but for unknown reasons Lord Raglan called for Captain Louis Nolan, one of Richard Airey's aides. We know Nolan was an excellent horseman and had written a book on cavalry tactics. He was an experienced officer with service in India, and so one of the officer types detested by Lord Cardigan.

Whether Lord Raglan knew of Nolan's bitterness and anger towards the commander of the cavalry division I doubt, but it was probably his skill as a horseman negotiating the steep, fifteen-minute descent into the north valley, that was Raglan's reasoning. As Nolan commenced a difficult descent towards the cavalry brigades below, the Russians at the far end of the valley composed themselves following their bashing from the Heavy Brigade. It was nearly an hour since that battle and the Russian survivors gathered at the very far end of north valley.

Close to the British cavalry, the French Chasseurs d'Afrique gathered; they amounted to 1,290 sabres, anxiously waiting to see if they would be deployed in support of Lord Lucan. Ahead of them, and to their right, stood the Light Brigade, roughly now in line with Redoubt 4. Captain Nolan found his way to the front of the Light Brigade, by then strung across the valley in two lines (three lines by the time they moved off).

Although Raglan's 4th order explicitly mentions guns (*follow the enemy and try to prevent the enemy carrying away the guns*), neither Lucan nor Cardigan could actually see Russians attempting to remove them from Redoubts 3, 2 and 1 – unlike Lord Raglan and his staff (including Nolan) on Sapoune Heights. Although those captured guns were hidden from view on the plain, both Lucan and Cardigan saw, in the distance, Cossack batteries crossing the valley at a range of about 1½ miles.

Taking the order from Nolan, Lucan read it. At once he saw the impracticability of the order for any useful purpose whatever, and thus the consequent great unnecessary risk and loss to be incurred. To Captain Nolan, Lucan expressed in no uncertain terms the uselessness of such an attack and the dangers attending it. Nolan, perhaps naturally, would not permit his commander-in-chief to be criticized by Lucan without some form of support. He reiterated the words of Raglan for the benefit of Lucan and staff officers gathered close by:

'Lord Raglan's orders are that the cavalry should attack immediately.'

Lord Lucan, now feeling impatient at the outburst from this staff captain, remarked loudly:

'Attack sir! Attack what? What guns, sir?'

He may have also uttered the words to Nolan 'where and what to do?' The impatient captain threw back his head and pointed with his hand in a direction Lucan said later was towards the left front part of the north valley.

'There my lord, is your enemy; there are your guns.'

Later, as we shall see in his speech to the House of Lords, Lord Lucan said that Nolan pointed to the 'further end of the valley,' but other than that his written version of events and that of his House of Lords speech more or less tally in detail. Nolan's words were delivered, Lucan says, in a most disrespectful but significant manner. His ADC, Captain Charles Pyndar Beauchamp Walker, described the delivery of the order as by an officer hostile to the general.

Captain Arthur Tremayne, sitting with the 13th Light Dragoons, describes Lucan's evident astonishment at the message and that Nolan pointed right down the valley. All witnesses so far indicate Nolan pointing to the far end of the valley. But in this Nolan was wrong. Despite being angered by Nolan's words, the commander of the cavalry division thought not to question things further. Mistakenly, he decided to accept the flung out hand of the irritating captain as the destination for his division; at the far end of the north valley.

Lord Lucan then selected the Light Brigade for the task; the Heavy Brigade was still too exhausted to undertake the order following their earlier charge. Riding off, Lucan went to Lord Cardigan, who sat on his horse in front of the 13th Light Dragoons; Nolan followed and asked his friend Captain Morris of the 17th if he could ride with them, and Morris agreed. What passed between the two senior men of the cavalry is generally in agreement. Lord Lucan imparted the contents of the 4th order, or at least its main tenor, short of handing the attack order to Cardigan, before telling the brigade commander to advance – although the word 'attack' was not mentioned.

Lord Cardigan's version is that he was ordered to attack the Russians in the valley about ¾ of a mile distant (actually about 1½ miles), with the 13th Light Dragoons and the 17th Lancers. Lord Lucan's version of events differs. After giving the order brought by Captain Nolan to Lord Cardigan (he does not mention handing him the written order), he urged his lordship to advance steadily and to keep his men well in hand (Cardigan said no such communication took place between him and Lucan).

Lucan's idea was that Cardigan was to use his discretion and act as circumstances might show themselves; by keeping his four squadrons (in fact five) under perfect control, he should have halted them as soon as he found that there was no useful object to be gained but great risk to be incurred. It was clearly his duty to handle his brigade as the Heavy Brigade had been handled earlier, to save them from unnecessary loss. Lord Lucan must have thought later that Lord Cardigan did not understand the task, judging by the way his brigade was fronting towards the end of the valley.

There were Russian guns facing him, so surely he must have understood that without attacking either of the enemy columns (Fedioukine Heights and Causeway Heights) he must run a distance between them for more than a mile, before being able to charge the more distant Russian battery. So upon hearing the words of his divisional commander, Lord Cardigan brought down his sword in salute to Lord Lucan and answered 'certainly sir; but allow me to point out to you that the Russians have a battery in the valley in our front and batteries and riflemen on each flank.'

Lord Lucan agreed with this, later believing that he thought Cardigan was only referring to those Russian forces up on the Fedioukine Heights. Accordingly, he shrugged his shoulders and replied 'I know it but Lord Raglan will have it. We have no choice but to obey.'

According to Cardigan, Lord Lucan replied 'I cannot help that; it is Lord Raglan's positive orders that the Light Brigade attacks immediately.'

Cardigan then signified his acceptance of this order and prepared for the advance by riding past his close staff and saying to Lord Paget from 4th Light Dragoons, who was waiting just ahead of the second line 'you will take command of the second line and I expect your best support – mind, your best support!'

Lord Paget replied 'of course, my lord, you shall have my best support!' Lord Lucan then began his usual interfering, albeit it in a sensitive way, to narrow the front of the brigade by moving the 11th Hussars from the front line and placing it in support in a second line, just behind 17th Lancers. The brigade moved off at about 11:10 a.m. Now, the narrowing of the front by Lord Lucan indicates one of two things: either the brigade was narrowed to protect the flanks from bombardment expected off Fedioukine and Causeway Heights, or it was narrowed to enable it to swarm up the Causeway Heights in an attempt to destroy those Russians bent on removing the captured British guns.

This is what Raglan wanted. Cardigan's behaviour was faultless, and described by Raglan as 'brave as a lion'. As the advance began, two regiments from the Heavy Brigade, led by Lucan, followed in support. Lord Cardigan's next order was 'draw swords,' and all the men held their weapons upright; the Lancers held lances at the 'carry.' Then followed his next order: 'the brigade will advance. First squadron of the 17th Lancers direct.'

The front of those first two regiments, just behind Cardigan, had a width of around 140 yards, with the men riding just about knee to knee. As the brigade began to advance, Lucan, now waiting at the head of the heavy regiments about to follow, must have had a premonition that the attack was likely to become a disaster, with the blame falling squarely upon him. He therefore handed Raglan's written 4th order to Sir John Blunt (his interpreter), who would not be accompanying the charge, for safe keeping. This advance must therefore be considered as a single operation; a charge by the Light Brigade with two regiments from the Heavy Brigade in support.

Two horse lengths to the front rode Cardigan on his chestnut horse, and it was to him that the front line following looked for guidance and the word of command; the second line would look to the front line for guidance, and the third line to the second line, and so forth. Behind Cardigan rode the brigade staff: Lieutenant Maxse, George Wombwell and Captain Lockwood; the whole brigade initially at a walk heading straight down the north valley towards the Russian guns in the distance, and almost in range of the first enemy guns on the surrounding heights.

They moved to a gentle trot, and after about 100 paces Lord Cardigan at the head was suddenly angered by the appearance on the scene of Captain Nolan, who crossed his front left to right. The man turned in his saddle, waved his sword and shouted something to those following Cardigan. The diagonal vector maintained by the captain must surely point the direction he believed the brigade was supposed to go; up the Causeway Heights near Redoubt 3? There can be little doubt that Nolan was trying to redirect the brigade towards Redoubt 3 and the Odessa Regiment stationed there, at a range of about 1200 yards – not the guns at the far end of the valley.

But the noise of a cavalry brigade on the move, however, would have cut out any verbal shouting made by Nolan; also, any verbal interceding by Captain Morris the moment Nolan veered off was lost upon Nolan. He, however, was the only person present then aware of the magnitude of the error being made by Cardigan.

'That won't do, Nolan!' Morris shouted, 'we've a long way to go and must be steady.'

Lord Cardigan saw the intervention by Nolan as an attempt to hurry the brigade forward, not an effort to veer the brigade to the right and up on the Causeway Heights. There was no time, however, for Nolan to steer back and advise Cardigan of the mistake, for one of the very first enemy artillery shells flew down to the right of the brigade commander and exploded near Nolan.

A shrapnel fragment hit him full in the chest and killed him instantly. His sword dropped but his carrying arm remained in the air. His frightened horse turned and galloped back to the approaching brigade; it was now that witnesses saw Nolan still sat upright in the saddle, and heard a scream so strange, appalling and unearthly. Lord Paget indicated that the front line had not moved very far when Captain Nolan suddenly realized the error of Cardigan's way and decided he had no choice but to intervene; a matter of a few hundred yards at the most before Nolan started off.

Whether the fatal explosion was aimed at the lead officer (Cardigan) or was just misguided is open to speculation; I believe the Russians were trying to find their range, and were aiming so that the rest of the front line of the brigade would be in Cardigan's position by the time the gunners on the Fedioukine Heights had time to reload. At the moment of Nolan's demise, the brigade was at a steady trot, which equates to about 8 mph. The guns on the Fedioukine Heights were only just alert as to what was happening in the valley below, but on the opposite side of the valley, at Redoubt 3, the Odessa Regiment saw the advancing cavalry and hastily abandoned their position.

The Russians on the heights must have stood incredulous at the sight of the enemy cavalry continuing to move with pace along the plain; they too probably expected to see the British veer off sharply to the right, but they did not, and this opportunity gave time to load their guns. Those on both sides of the valley now opened fire and found their range. Gaps suddenly appeared in the ranks that were quickly closed as men rode towards centre ground. The neat lines of the initial advance started to become ragged and almost uncontrollable. It was important that officers kept their men together for the final charge.

Despite cannon fire from both sides, the advance remained at a settled pace dictated by Lord Cardigan in the lead; as explosions started to play havoc and horses became jumpy, it was difficult to remain in control. Several officers found themselves riding almost alongside Lord Cardigan, and were told by him not to force the pace in no uncertain terms! Except for these incidents, Cardigan did not make a sign or utter any other words – neither did he look back to see the state of the troops following him.

Lord Cardigan, however, still rode stiff and erect in the saddle of his horse, and stuck rigidly to the cavalry rules: trot until within 250 yards of the enemy, gallop until within 40-50 yards of the target, and thereafter charge, at full speed. Cardigan increased pace, since the regiment following was almost upon him; all the men behind realized that their commander was heading straight for the mouth of the guns. It made sense now to get amongst those guns as soon as possible and finish the job

At about 80 yards from them at full gallop, the Cossack battery let loose a devastating salvo at the brigade. Lord Cardigan and his survivors thundered through the smoke of the gun line, and on to the Russian cavalry gathered on the other side. For more detail of the following battle from arrival at the guns, see volume II of this work. I will concentrate more now on Lord Cardigan, with a bit of Lucan thrown in out of necessity. So, back to the charge.

There was no support, as promised by Lord Raglan, other than the French Chasseurs d'Afrique racing up the Fedioukine Heights to attack the Russian artillery pounding the north valley. Where was the Heavy Brigade and Lord Lucan, who had been following at the off? The Heavy Brigade was taking hits. Colonel John Yorke of the 1st Royals lost his horse and then had his left leg shattered; Lucan was hit in the leg and an aide-de-camp, Captain Walker Charteris, was killed.

Injuries would have been more severe had it not been for intervention by the French cavalry on the left flank. The Heavy Brigade instead turned around and abandoned the Light Brigade to its fate. As they went about, Lord Lucan turned to Lord William Paulet, assistant adjutant-general of the cavalry division, and spoke in carefully shrouded words 'they have sacrificed the Light Brigade,' he said, 'they shall not have the heavies if I can help it!'

I think we must conclude when he uttered to Lord Paulet, that the Light Brigade was by then reaching the guns, and that he believed they would be destroyed and were lost. Not wanting to lose the other half of his division, naturally, to some senseless order from Lord Raglan, Lucan made the decision to turn about – he could, of course, have queried the order by sending an aide to Lord Raglan for clarification, but that would have taken more time. But what lives it could have saved.

During all the mass confusion and utter chaos at the opposite end of the valley, Lord Cardigan continued into the smoke beyond the guns and soon found himself alone, approaching a large mass of retreating Russian cavalry. These stopped quickly and turned about again. Lord Cardigan stopped briskly and found himself but twenty yards from the enemy. The two eyed each other up for a few moments; the grey coated Russian Cossacks with teeth clenched and the top representative of Britain, dressed in his gold pelisse.

Two Cossacks approached Cardigan and suggested he surrender. When he made no effort to obey they set about him with their lances, but he remained upright in the saddle with his sword at the slope. During this brief tussle, Lord Cardigan received a wound to the hip; the Cossacks, now aware that the British cavalry was arriving and their colleagues were getting ready to withdraw, likewise followed suite. Lord Cardigan had an opportunity to retreat, and this he did.

The charge of the Light Brigade still raged beyond the Russian guns but, unable to see this through the smoke and seeing only the backs of some of his front line retreating, Lord Cardigan probably believed there was nothing left for him to usefully do. He decided to leave with the rest, for he could not see either his supports, who should have been following: 11th Hussars, 4th Light Dragoons and the 8th Hussars. It never occurred to Cardigan, it seems, that they could still be behind the Russian guns, hacking their way ahead, as indeed they were.

This lapse of thought for the rest of his brigade leads many historians to believe Cardigan thought more of his own personal safety over that of his command. Nevertheless, in the confusion of the moment the Light Brigade leader started a slow retreat alone from the scene of carnage. He could have also, of course, raced back to Lucan and demanded support to help extricate his brigade from the jaws of hell, but instead other things were on his mind. He soon arrived back at the position where Scarlett sat with his Heavy Brigade.

Lucan denies that he was present at the time, but only when the last of the Light Brigade returned to safety. Not unsurprisingly, Cardigan's first sentences were uttered against the officer who had rode across the front of the brigade at the onset of the advance. General Scarlett pointed out that his lordship had almost ridden over Nolan's dead body. According to Scarlett, this conversation took place just after he pointed out to Lord Lucan a body of cavalry, which he describes as being from 4th Light Dragoons and 11th Hussars, retreating on the Fedioukine Heights side of the valley.

This indicates that Lord Lucan was there when Lord Cardigan returned from the charge. Lord Paget was one of the last to get to safety due to his tired horse. Here he was met by Cardigan. Paget exclaimed to the brigade commander 'Holloa! Lord Cardigan, weren't you there?' Those with the earl smiled, but Cardigan was perhaps less amused. 'Wasn't I though?' he replied, turning to Captain Jenyns at his side and saying 'here Jenyns; did not you see me at the guns?'

Jenyns replied that he had seen Lord Cardigan, as he was near him at the time. Paget then asked of the 17th Lancers and 13th Light Dragoons, of whom he had seen little during the fight. 'I am afraid there are no such regiments in existence as the 13th and the 17th, for I can give no account of them,' Cardigan said. Paget then saw a group of lancers nearby with their horses – since there was but one lancer regiment in the Crimea, these had to be survivors of the 17th.

The charge of the Light Brigade lasted approximately half an hour, from commencement to last stragglers arriving to safety. The cheers continued as more and more men, mostly on foot, arrived in the area of the Heavy Brigade. After a short while, the survivors were assembled and Lord Cardigan addressed them. 'Men,' he said, 'it is a mad brained trick, but it is no fault of mine.' Other reports suggest Cardigan said 'men, it is a great blunder, but it is no fault of mine.'

Nevertheless, someone amongst the survivors replied 'never-mind my Lord; we are ready to go again,' to which Lord Cardigan replied 'no, no men! You have done enough.' When roll muster was complete, Lord Cardigan rode up to Lord Raglan, who by now with his staff had descended into the north valley, to report. Both men must have been seething with anger during this meeting.

In what was described by attendant witnesses as a severe and angry exchange. Lord Raglan, shaking with rage more than his staff had ever seen before, said 'what did you mean, sir, by attacking a battery in front, contrary to all the usages of warfare and the customs of the service?' Cardigan's indignant reply was 'my Lord, I hope you will not blame me, for I received the order to attack from my superior officer in front of the troops.' He then proceeded to relate the part he had taken in the battle, and the narrative convinced Lord Raglan of the correctness of Cardigan's actions.

In correspondence a few days later, Lord Raglan described Cardigan as having acted with great steadiness, gallantry and perseverance. A short time later, Lord Raglan came upon Lord Lucan and said to him 'you have lost the Light Brigade!' Lord Lucan's reply was to deny he had lost the brigade, and that he was only carrying out the orders, written and verbal, conveyed to him by Captain Nolan. Surprisingly, Lord Raglan did not have a copy on his person of either his 3rd or 4th orders issued that day! Lucan held the original order, written by

General Richard Airey. Instead of querying it at this stage, Raglan replied, according to the divisional commander, 'Lord Lucan, you were a lieutenant general and should therefore have exercised your discretion and not approving of the charge, should not have caused it to be made.'

Lord Lucan could counter this easily, because Raglan, from his location on the Sapoune Heights, had a much better view of the valley below than those actually below in it; to disobey such an order from the commander-in-chief who had superior knowledge of the situation was not possible. Not even Cardigan, Lucan nor Nolan could see the attempt at removing the guns on the Causeway Heights by the Russians; only those on the Sapoune Heights saw what was going on, if indeed the Russians were trying to remove them.

13. WHAT LORD LUCAN SAID

A note to General Airey

Explanatory statements were made numerous times by Lord Lucan for the disaster, both to private individuals and to those with a vested interest in hearing his explanations. His first business on the day following the tragedy was to write a brief note to General Airey, enclosing a copy of the order handed to him by Captain Nolan on the battlefield. Having had Lord Raglan blame him for the charge shortly after the remains of the Light Brigade returned to safety, Lucan was anxious that Raglan, having given the order his attention, should not still think 'I lost the Light Brigade in that unfortunate incident,' as he describes it. [1]

Lucan's letter of 30th November 1854

By the 30th November, Lucan was writing his explanations direct to Raglan, being now aware that Raglan's report of 28th October to the Secretary of State was being published in British newspapers back home. In Raglan's letter, he said that the enemy withdrew from ground momentarily occupied (*Redoubts 1 – 3, with no mention at this stage by Raglan of captured British guns also being withdrawn* – my thoughts are now in brackets and italics). [2] His lordship continued that he ordered the cavalry to advance, supported by Cathcart's 4th Division, and to take any opportunity to regain the heights. This could not be carried out immediately (*due to the slow pace and reluctance of George Cathcart to advance into the north valley*).

But once it appeared that the Russians were attempting to remove captured British guns, Lord Raglan desired that Lucan advance rapidly, follow the enemy in their retreat and try to prevent them from effecting their objective (*that being the differences here between his orders of the day no. 3 and 4*). Meanwhile, the Russians had reformed on their own ground with artillery in front and on the flanks (*this following their defeat to the Heavy Brigade earlier that morning*). Lord Raglan continued in his letter to the Secretary of State that, under some misconception of the instruction to advance, the lieutenant general (*Lord Lucan*) considered that he was bound to attack at all hazards, and accordingly ordered the Earl of Cardigan to move forward with the Light Brigade. (*Here clearly the blame, from Raglan's point of view, lies squarely on Lord Lucan's 'misconception' of the order delivered by Captain Nolan*).

Raglan goes on to say that the order was obeyed in the most spirited and gallant manner, and that Lord Cardigan charged with the upmost vigour to attack a battery firing upon the advancing squadrons and, having passed beyond it, engaged the Russian cavalry in the rear. But there, Lord Cardigan's troops were also assailed by enemy artillery, infantry and cavalry, and out of necessity retired, having committed so much havoc upon the enemy. Lord Lucan's letter of 30th November speaks immediately of Raglan's view that he (*Lord Lucan*) was under some misconception of the instruction to advance, and considered that he was bound to attack at all hazards; that Lord Raglan's assumption was a grave charge and imputation reflecting seriously on Lucan's professional character.

Lord Lucan could remain silent no more, he said – it was, he felt, incumbent on him to state facts which he could not doubt, would clear him of these unmerited accusations. Lord Lucan had the cavalry lined up to support an intended movement of infantry (*Cathcart's 4th Division and Raglan's 3rd order*) when Captain Nolan arrived at speed with the written instruction (*which he then included a copy within the text of his letter*). Having read carefully the order he hesitated and went on to urge the uselessness of such an attack and the dangers attending it; that the aide (*Nolan*) in a most authoritative tone, stated that they were Lord Raglan's orders that the cavalry should attack immediately.

Lucan asked Nolan where and what to do, as neither enemy nor guns were within sight, to which Nolan replied in a most disrespectful but significant manner, pointing to the far end of the valley and saying 'there my lord is your enemy; there are your guns.' [3] Lord Lucan goes on to say that Lord Raglan's instructions were so distinct and the urging so positive of the aide that he felt it imperative to obey, and informed Lord Cardigan to advance despite Cardigan's objections, to which Lord Lucan agreed entirely but stated that they were his lordship's (*Raglan's*) orders. Lord Lucan, despite his convictions, then proceeded to render the charge as little perilous as possible, by adding the support of two regiments of heavy cavalry, the Scots Greys and the Royals.

These he halted during the advance when they reached the spot from which they could protect the retreat of the light cavalry in the event of them being pursued by the enemy and also when, having lost many officers and men from the fire of batteries and forts (*redoubts*), further advance would have exposed them to destruction. Lord Lucan considered it the only course open to him at the time, and that as a lieutenant general he had discretionary powers, but to take them upon himself would be to disobey an order written by the commander-in-chief (*Raglan*) within a few minutes of its delivery.

Also, that the order had been given from Lord Raglan's elevated position (*on Sapoune Heights*), where he commanded an entire view of all the batteries and the position of the enemy, but Lord Lucan considered it would have been nothing less than direct disobedience of orders without any other reason than that he preferred his own opinion to that of his general (*Raglan*). In this instance, it must have exposed him (*Lucan*) and the cavalry to aspersions against which it might have been difficult to have defended themselves.

(*This last paragraph tends to lend weight to the fact that Lord Lucan believed Lord Raglan, from his position on the Sapoune Heights, could see enemy positions better than Lucan could from the north valley, and therefore he had no choice but to obey the order, assuming that the order and the demonstration by Captain Nolan pointing to the far end of the north valley, were of course correct*).

Lord Lucan then described how the aide sent (*Nolan*), was well informed of his general's intentions (*Raglan – presumably since Nolan had been on the Sapoune Heights before delivering the order*), and first insisted on an immediate charge before taking position in front of one of the leading squadrons, where subsequently he fell the first victim. Lord Lucan therefore dared not disobey Lord Raglan's order, and it was the opinion of every officer of rank in the army to whom he had shown Lord Raglan's written instructions, that it was not possible for him to disobey (*by exercising his discretion as a lieutenant general*).

He ended the letter asking for Lord Raglan's justice, as he was sensitively anxious to satisfy his sovereign, his military superiors and the public that he had not, on this unhappy occasion, shown himself undeserving of their confidence or unfitting the command that he held.

Raglan's letter 16th December to secretary of state

Naturally, Lord Raglan felt compelled to forward a copy of the Lucan letter to his superior the Duke of Newcastle on 16th December 1854 (*this was received by Pelham-Clinton, Secretary of State for War at that time, on 8th January 1855, or 23 days later*). Firstly he regretted that it was necessary for him to forward the letter in the first place! Lucan's letter was at first handed to Richard Airey, with instructions to suggest to Lord Lucan that he withdraw the communication, since it would not lead to his advantage in the slightest degree. [4] This Lord Lucan refused to do. Lord Raglan declared to the duke that Lucan had not only misconceived the written instruction sent him, but that there was nothing in the instruction which called upon him to attack at all hazards, or to undertake the operation which led to such a brilliant display of gallantry on the part of the Light Brigade, with its lamentable casualties in every regiment.

Continuing, Lord Raglan said that Lord Lucan was wholly silent with respect to his previous order sent to him. **'Cavalry to advance and take advantage of any opportunity to recover the heights. They will be supported by the infantry which have been ordered. Advance on two fronts.'** Lord Raglan believed that this 3rd order to the cavalry had not been attended to by Lord Lucan; it was as a result of this that the 4th order was delivered to him by Captain Nolan (**Lord Raglan wishes the cavalry to advance rapidly to the front – follow the enemy and try to prevent the enemy carrying away the guns – troop horse artillery may accompany – French cavalry is on your left (signed R Airey) immediate**).

Lord Raglan believed that Lord Lucan had read the order (*the 3rd order*) with very little attention, for he was now stating that the cavalry was formed up to support the infantry, whereas he had been told by Richard Airey that they were to advance and take advantage of any opportunity to recover the heights and that they would be supported by infantry. The result of Lucan's inattention was that he had no men in advance of his main body of men, made no attempt to regain the heights, and was so little informed of the position of the enemy that he asked Captain Nolan where and what to attack, since neither enemy nor guns were in sight.

This was admitted by Lord Lucan. His inattention to the first order (*3rd order*) never occurred to him that it might be connected to the second order (*4th order*) and that it was a repetition of the first. It was viewed by Lord Lucan as a positive order to attack at all hazards, whereas Richard Airey's note did not mention the word 'attack' at all. Thus Lord Lucan was prepared to attack an unseen enemy, whose position, numbers and composition he was wholly unacquainted with, and whom, in consequence of a previous order, he had taken no steps whatever to watch. Lord Raglan adds that he undoubtedly had no intention that Lucan should make such an attack, and that there was nothing in the instruction requiring it.

Lord Raglan continued that he wished he could say that Lord Lucan, having decided against his conviction to make the movement, did all he could to render it as little perilous as possible, but this, in Lord Raglan's judgment, was far from being the case. Lord Lucan was told that horse artillery might accompany the cavalry; he did not bring it up. He was informed that the French cavalry was on his left; he did not invite their co-operation. He had the whole of the heavy cavalry at his disposal; he brought only two regiments in support, but omits all other precautions, either from want of due consideration, or from supposition that the unseen enemy was not in such a great force as he apprehended, notwithstanding that he was warned of it by Lord Cardigan after he had received the order to attack.

Lord Raglan did not, he admits to the Secretary of State for War, wish to disparage the Earl of Lucan, nor to cast a slur upon his professional reputation – but having been accused of things unmerited in his dispatches (*3rd and 4th orders to Lord Lucan*), he felt obliged to enter into the subject with the secretary and trouble him at more length than he could have wished.

Letter from Newcastle to Raglan dated 27th Jan 1855

Henry Pelham-Clinton, Secretary of State for War at the time, wrote back to Lord Raglan on 27th January 1855, having received Raglan's communique regarding Lord Lucan. Raglan's despatch, with that of Lucan, was forwarded immdiately to Viscount Hardinage, the army commander-in-chief. An extract of guidance from the viscount, received by Pelham-Clinton on the 26th January, was enclosed for Lord Raglan's attention; this had been forwarded and approved by Queen Victoria herself! Lord Raglan was therefore instructed to inform Lord Lucan that he should resign his command and return to England. Other than this extract, Newcastle purposely made no further comments to Lord Raglan regarding Lord Lucan. The suggestion that he should be recalled was that of the Duke of Newcastle, and of course, Viscount Hardinage approved it.

Letter to Lord Lucan from Lord Raglan

A letter from Lord Raglan dated 13th February 1855 to Lord Lucan relayed the contents of Newcastle's letter of 27th January; Raglan found it, he said, a painful duty but he made no further comments about the content, other than offering to see Lord Lucan if he so wished.

Letter to Adjutant General in London from Lord Lucan

Lord Lucan wrote to the Army adjutant general on 2nd March 1855, announcing that he had obeyed Her Majesties request that he resign command of the cavalry in the east, and that he had returned to England. He seized the earliest moment to request a courts martial into his conduct in ordering the charge of the light cavalry, and that of the cotents of his letter to Lord Raglan of the 30th instance. He believed it to be an undoubted privilage for any soldier when their conduct had been unjustly impugned.

Letter from Horse Guards to Lord Lucan dated 5th March

A reply to Lord Lucan's letter of 2nd March was received by his lordship three days later, on the 5th instance, from G A Wetherall, adjutant general. He was directed by the commander-in-chief to state in reply that, after a careful review of the whole correspondence passed, he could not recommend to Her Majesty that his lordship's conduct be investigated by courts martial. Lord Lucan wrote back the same day, indicating that he was not in possession of all the facts at the time of Lord Raglan's original letter to the minister of war, and that the letter contained entirely new matter and new charges reflecting more seriously than before on his professional judgement and character.

(*These items included: the fact that Lord Lucan was told that horse artillery might accompany the cavalry and he did not bring it up; he was informed that the French cavalry was on his left but he did not invite their co-operation, and he also had the whole of the heavy cavalry at his disposal, but he brought only two regiments in support, etc.*)

These charges Lord Lucan considered so grave that they could not be properly disposed of without military investigation; therefore, he was compelled to express his anxious wish that the commander-in-chief kindly reconsider his decision and consent to a courts martial. On 12th March 1855 G A Wetherall replied to Lord Lucan – the commander-in-chief would not change his decision, and there would not be any courts martial.

Lord Lucan's opinions

Lord Lucan therefore was not to be given the opportunity he believed his right to clear his name through official army channels. This did not stop him from expounding his views to other people, both in the Crimea and back home, and one of those eager to question him was Alexander Kinglake, historian and writer who was there at the time of various battles and keen to interview those participating. Much of Kinglake's source was also letters sent him by W G Romaine, who was attached to British Headquarters staff as judge advocate; also, Kinglake was there at the battle of the Alma and Lord Raglan himself suggested to him that he write a history of the Crimean War, and so made available all his private papers! During one such interview with Lord Lucan, various questions arose to which his lordship gave his opinion.

How did the enemy manage to establish their batteries on the heights in the first place?

Lord Lucan said that it was not possible for Colin Campbell to prevent the enemy establishing themselves on the heights commanding the village of Kamara, being far from his base (*Kadikoi*) and requiring a strong force of infantry and artillery. The army had been obliged to stop patrolling the area a full week before the charge of the Light Brigade, as the enemy was occupying Tchorgoun village and high ground between it and Kamara (*lack of patrols perhaps indicate how the Russians were able to keep quiet their intentions in the Balaclava valley*).

What grounds were there for cavalry to avoid attacking the forces which assailed the Turkish Redoubts? (*These being redoubts 1 – 3, of course, near Kamara.*)

Lord Lucan said that Lord Raglan had not acted upon the communication sent him the day before by Sir Colin Campbell, nor when he himself informed Raglan of the approach of a considerable Russian army. There was no support, and Lord Lucan and Sir Colin considered it first their duty to defend the approach to Balaclava. They also considered that the cavalry would be used chiefly for the defence of the town, and so they were moved into reserve for that purpose.

The redoubts were only left when they had been captured by the enemy. Lord Lucan was thus of the opinion that any enemy advance on Balaclava could only be resisted by our cavalry on the plain. The soundness of his opinion was established by the check and retreat of the enemy cavalry on the site he had prepared to meet them (*this being the land east of the vineyard, during the charge of the Heavy Brigade*).

Was it a surprise when Russian cavalry turned to engage the Heavy Brigade?

This, Lord Lucan said, was no surprise. The enemy entering the valley moved very slow, and should have been seen by General Scarlett from the distance of one mile. Lucan himself saw them before they crowned the heights, and found time enough to travel over double the extent of the ground and to halt, form and dress the attacking line before the enemy had traversed half the breadth of the valley.

What grounds were there for the Heavy Brigade to desist from supporting the Light Brigade in its charge?

This was an important question, for which Lord Lucan was to be severely criticised over time. His lordship replied firstly that he had divided the Light Brigade from two lines to three, to expose as few men as possible in the first line and to sufficiently support it. (*A reasonable thing to do, in my opinion, but proof clearly by that stage that both Lucan and Cardigan were intending to attack the far end of the north valley, as opposed to the Causeway Heights as required by Lord Raglan*). As soon as they moved off, Lord Lucan instructed his ADC to have the Heavy Brigade follow him, divided in three similar lines to that of the Light Brigade.

He then galloped off after Cardigan, but when quite far down the valley observed that the Heavy Brigade in his rear was suffering severely from flanking batteries. Realizing that they were already sufficiently close to protect the Light Brigade should they be pursued by the enemy and that he could not allow the heavies to be sacrificed as had been the Light Brigade, he caused them to halt. Had not the French Chasseurs d'Afrique silenced some of those batteries, it was Lord Lucan's opinion that the heavies would have been destroyed. When halted, there was no possible object for further exposing them, and that they could only be useful in protecting the retreat of the Light Brigade – this they materially did.

(*Interestingly, Lord Lucan describes the 'sacrifice of the Light Brigade' – indicating that he (and probably Cardigan) interpreted Raglan's 4th order as likely leading to the destruction of the Light Brigade*).

The purport of the order given to Lord Cardigan after receipt of the order brought by Captain Nolan?

Carrying Lord Raglan's 4th order in his hand, Lord Lucan trotted over to Lord Cardigan at the head of his brigade. He then gave Lord Cardigan distinctly its contents, so far as they concerned him: 'Lord Raglan wishes the cavalry to advance rapidly to the front – follow the enemy and try to prevent the enemy carrying away the guns – troop horse artillery may accompany – French cavalry is on your left (signed R Airey) immediate.' (*Possibly the last lines, 'troop horse artillery may accompany – French cavalry is on your left (signed R Airey) immediate' were not given to Lord Cardigan, although I feel that they did concern him significantly.*) Lord Cardigan objected at once, on the ground that he would be exposed to a flanking battery. When ordered to take up position, he had continued to express through his ADC the same apprehensions. Lucan told Cardigan that he was aware of it, but Lord Raglan would have it and that they had no choice but to obey. Lord Lucan then told Cardigan that he wished him to advance very steadily and quietly and that he would narrow his front by removing the 11th Hussars from the first to the second line. This Lord Cardigan strenuously opposed, but Lord Lucan moved across his front and directed Colonel Douglas not to advance with the rest of the line, but to form a second line with the 4th Light Dragoons.

14. WHAT LORD CARDIGAN SAID

On 5th December 1854, citing ill-health, Lord Cardigan set off for England a good number of weeks before his superior officer, Lord Lucan, was sacked and recalled home. In such circumstances, the word of an officer regarding fitness to serve would normally be accepted by the senior officer commanding, but Lord Raglan only permitted his departure after a medical board had confirmed the claimed disability!

Statement by Lord Cardigan

Explanatory statements were also made many times by Lord Cardigan for the disaster, both to private individuals and to those with a vested interest in hearing his explanations. Alexander Kinglake, the noted historical writer, was one of these and a statement was laid before him. According to Lord Cardigan, the brigade was suddenly ordered to mount up, upon which he sent an aide to reconnoitre the ground ahead. Lord Lucan then rode to the front of his brigade and spoke.

'Lord Cardigan, you will attack the Russians in the valley,' he said.

'Certainly my lord,' Cardigan replied, lowering his sword in salute, 'but allow me to point out to you that there is a battery in front, a battery on each flank, and the ground is covered with Russian riflemen.'

'I cannot help that,' Lord Lucan replied, 'it is Lord Raglan's positive order that the Light Brigade is to attack the enemy.' Upon this, Lord Lucan ordered the 11th Hussars back to support the 17th Lancers.

(Here Lord Lucan uses phrases not from the written 4th order: Lord Raglan's positive order that the Light Brigade is to attack the enemy – how Lord Lucan could misinterpret the 4th order cannot be beyond a reasonable doubt, for it only said to advance rapidly to the front and follow the enemy. However, to advance rapidly to the front would take the Light Brigade directly to the far end of the north valley, because the enemy on Redoubts 1 – 3 could not be seen from the location of the Light Brigade. What would have been the result had Lord Lucan handed the 4th order to Lord Cardigan for him to read and interpret?

'Lord Raglan wishes the cavalry to advance rapidly to the front – follow the enemy and try to prevent the enemy carrying away the guns – troop horse artillery may accompany – French cavalry is on your left (signed R Airey) immediate.'

Surely Lord Cardigan would have raised these four objections had he read the order: follow the enemy – what and where the enemy? Try to prevent the enemy carrying away the guns – what and where the guns? Troop horse artillery may accompany – what and where the troop horse artillery and why would horse artillery accompany an attack? Lastly, French cavalry is on your left – what and where the French cavalry? Since they could not see any enemy nor guns to follow, how could the Light Brigade carry out this part of the order? Also, where was the troop horse artillery; where was the French cavalry on the left, and who was to lead them during the attack – the French commander on the ground, or Lord Cardigan?

There is enough confusion with the text of Lord Raglan's 4th order to enable Lord Lucan to seek clarification. A lieutenant general would surely not seek just the advice from a mere captain (Nolan)? The regulations would require, in the event of unclear orders, for clarification to be sought, either in person or by sending an ADC to find the originator. This, of course, could not happen for two reasons: firstly, the 4th order stated quite clearly to advance rapidly and, after General Airey's signature, the word immediate (although this could also mean immediate delivery of the written order); secondly, it would take about fifteen minutes for the ADC to find Lord Raglan, clarify the order, and then another fifteen minutes to return to Lords Lucan and Cardigan – more than half an hour wasted).

Lord Cardigan had led his brigade forward about eighty or one hundred yards when a shell fell close to his horse's feet; Captain Nolan was next seen riding across the front, retreating into the intervals (*between the regimental lines*) with his arm up (*Lord Cardigan mentions Captain Nolan no more for now*). He led the brigade down to the battery without seeing anybody in front of him, although he had to restrain some of the officers during the last eighty yards as they had become excited by the heavy fire. He led the charge into the battery, during which a shot was fired from one of the larger Russian guns close to his right leg.

He continued to lead the brigade through the Russian limber carriages and the ammunition wagons in the rear. When within twenty yards of the Russian cavalry, Lord Cardigan was attacked by two Cossack fighters, who wounded him slightly, but he made good his escape. Riding back to the gun battery, he could not see any part of the brigade so he rode slowly up the hill until he met General Scarlett, of whom he asked his opinion of the aide (*Nolan*) who had brought the order that had destroyed the Light Brigade, riding to the rear and screaming like a woman?

Scarlett replied to say no more, as he had ridden over his body. Lord Lucan was present when this was said. Lord Cardigan then rode over to the start position where he found his brigade gathered and a head count was taken; there were 195 mounted men out of 670 left. He then rode and found Lord Raglan, who said to him 'what do you mean, sir, by attacking a battery in front, contrary to all the usages of warfare and the custom of the service?' To this Lord Cardigan replied 'my lord, I hope you will not blame me, for I received the order to attack from my superior officer in front of the troops.' He then went on to describe what he had done during the charge to Lord Raglan. [5]

A further statement by Lord Cardigan

A later statement by Lord Cardigan was made to a series of queries historian Alexander Kinglake put to his lordship prior to publication of Kinglake's volumes about the Crimean war; the historian wanted to give ample room for Lord Cardigan to refute many of the stories and whispers that had built up over the years regarding his lordship's role in the charge of the Light Brigade. To begin, Lord Cardigan stated that the time taken from the commencement of the attack movement to reforming on the same ground did not exceed twenty minutes.

(It is unlikely, I would think, that any of the men involved from the brigade would check their pocket watches before and after an attack – most likely, this was an approximation of time, or else someone not involved with the charge but watching events recorded a time. During the battle of the Little Bighorn in 1876 (my work Clearing Reno, volumes 1 – 5 for more detail)

there were wild discrepancies in timing and very few men, probably only a couple from Reno's court of inquiry, actually checked their pocket watches, which is understandable during a pitched battle).

The distance covered during the charge was 1¼ miles and 300 men were killed, wounded or missing, including 24 officers, along with 396 horses killed (*equating to 59% of brigade horses, according to Lord Cardigan in the late 1860's*). His lordship presumed that nobody could doubt that he led the first line of the charge through the Russian battery, and as far as the Russian cavalry. Here he found himself alone and confronted by two Cossacks, on account of his staff being wounded or disabled.

Being slightly wounded by these Cossacks (*these Russians carried lances, of course*), gradually he retreated back to the line of the first guns, where he found himself alone again. Those members of the brigade who had survived had passed off to the left of the gun limber carriages, or retreated back up the hill. Cardigan swears upon his solemn oath that from his position he could see none of the first line nor the supports, who ought to have followed him in the attack but instead had diverged left and right.

(*Mainly true, with 8ᵗʰ Hussars (Shewell) diverting to the right of the enemy guns and 11ᵗʰ Hussars (Douglas) and 4ᵗʰ Light Dragoons (Paget) diverting to the left of them – the 4ᵗʰ particularly engaging the Russian guns there*).

The first line, according to Cardigan, did not follow him through the guns but instead, as he confronted those two Cossacks, passed to his left to avoid the Russian limber carriages; the loss of his staff for varying reasons meant he found himself completely alone. Thus his lordship asks was it not his duty to retreat gradually and slowly in rear of the broken parties of the first line up the hill, rather than turn and ride through Russian cavalry in search of his supports without knowing, at the time, which way they had gone; the supports having not followed the first line as they should have done?

It was his opinion that it was quite sufficient for a general of brigade to return with, as well as lead the attack of the front line unless, by chance, he should come in contact with his supports, in which case he would remain with them. It must be observed, Lord Cardigan believed, that no general officer could have rendered any service or assistance like that of Balaclava, in which all the losses of men and horses took just twenty minutes, and in which there were no troops left to attack overwhelming enemy forces. His lordship stated that it took eight minutes for the advance, eight minutes to retreat leaving just four minutes for fighting or collision with the enemy. The only point to consider, he believed, was whether he was justified in returning slowly in rear of his retreating line?

Evidence of proof appended to above statement

Lord Cardigan added an appendage of proof to his statement as further evidence that he had done all could during the charge, and only retreated because the three regiments of his supports had diverted and disappeared. Amongst the additions were the following:

1/ an extract from Colonel Jenyns' evidence (*Captain Jenyns of the 13ᵗʰ Hussars, who later took command after the deaths of Captains Oldham and Goad during the charge*), that Jenyns, along with one or two others, tried to rally the few men seen still mounted, but it was utterly impossible to do so and therefore they returned in broken detachments through the guns which were then deserted.

2/ from Lord Cardigan's own evidence: that no general officer could have been of any use; that the feeble remains of the lines of the brigade could have done nothing more under a general officer than they did under their own officers.

3/ from the evidence of Trumpet-Major William Gray (*8th Hussars*) that the Earl of Cardigan led the charge against the Russian battery at the head of the first line of the brigade; that the 8th Hussars and 4th Light Dragoons formed the rear line of the brigade but very early in the charge they became gradually separated, with the 8th Hussars bearing to the right and 4th Light Dragoons to the left – as they advanced farther, the distance between the two regiments increased very materially.

(*These two regiments were the supports that Lord Cardigan frequently refers too, the other being the 11th Hussars*).

4/ an extract from a letter written by Lord George Paget (*commanding 4th Light Dragoons*) to HRH the Duke of Cambridge (*1st infantry division*) in 1856: that on the advance of the first line, Lord Paget gave the command that the 'second line will advance; 4th Light Dragoons direct.'

(*I would query this statement because there were in fact three lines – perhaps the second line (11th Hussars) gave the impression to Paget that there was only one long line in front of his regiment (17th Lancers and 13th Hussars were the first line) or that he did not notice Lord Lucan's interfering by moving the 11th from the front line to reduce the width of the brigade*).

Soon into the advance he perceived that 8th Hussars (*on his right*) were bearing away to the right, and they kept losing their intervals and by the same process, their alignment, until finally they became completely separated. An officer named Lieutenant Martin was despatched to assist Colonel Shewell.

(*I often wonder how this evidence supports Lord Cardigan's decision to retreat from the battlefield, but since he states he could not find the supports, this is the reason why – they had diverted well to the left/right of the Russian guns, whereas Lord Cardigan was in the middle and during all the smoke and chaos, he could not see the 4th/8th in action on the flanks*).

5/ General Scarlett stated, in a letter to Colonel Calthorpe dated 1st May 1863, that at the instant the Light Brigade charged into the battery, it was almost impossible due to smoke and confusion, to discover what took place; but a few minutes afterwards, he observed the remnants of the Light Brigade as well as the second line retreating towards the ground occupied immediately before the charge.

(*Again there is confusion here regarding the second/third lines of the brigade and besides, since he was not with the charge much of which General Scarlett states must surely be inadmissible hearsay?*).

Dismounted men and horses without riders were scattered all over the space taken by the brigade during the advance. General Scarlett also remembered pointing out to Lord Cardigan the broken remnants of his line as they were retreating up the hill. Scarlett firmly believed from information he received at the time of the engagement and afterwards, that Lord Cardigan was the first to charge into the battery and that he was amongst the last, if not the last, to return from behind the guns of the first line of the brigade (*not the entire brigade*).

6/ Lieutenant George Johnson of 13th Hussars stated that they ought to have reformed but that there were none to reform had it been possible; his own regiment turned out 112 of all ranks and lost 84 horses (*75% of the regiment that morning*) – in fact, there were just 10 men assembled at the start position, with 26 wounded, 13 taken prisoner and 12 killed. Therefore, all the generals in the Crimea would have puzzled how to reform them.

Cardigan *v* Lieutenant Colonel Calthorpe

This court case came about as a result of comments made in a book *Letters from a Staff Officer in the Crimea,* published first in 1856 by Somerset John Gough Calthorpe, 7th Baron Calthorpe, and an aide-de-camp to Lord Raglan at the time of the charge of the Light Brigade. Somerset Calthorpe substantially maintained that Lord Cardigan retreated prematurely after the charge of the brigade, and also retreated without actually entering the enemy battery! In 1863, therefore, Lord Cardigan applied to the Queen's Bench for criminal information (*libel*) against Calthorpe. Affidavits were presented in support of Lord Cardigan entering the battery and riding some distance beyond. Calthorpe's response was that he now accepted Lord Cardigan entering beyond the Russian guns, but not the fact that the earl retreated prematurely – Calthorpe's book says this was the moment when a general was most required, but unfortunately Lord Cardigan was not then present. [6] To support this contention, Calthorpe adduced a mass of evidence which showed that, whilst 4th Light Dragoons/8th Hussars were advancing towards the battery, Lord Cardigan rode by on his way to the rear; to support this further, an affidavit from Lord Lucan said the same!

(*In fairness to Lord Cardigan, we should remember that the first line, that he led, was first into the guns before the 4th/8th had actually arrived on the flanks – although the time gap must have been quite small but enough, in my opinion, for Lord Cardigan to ride forward a few hundred yards, come across two aggressive Cossacks who wounded him with their lances, and for his lordship to decide to retreat to the gun battery where he could not, in the smoke, noise and confusion, see his supports. Remember also that Lord Lucan was not actually on the scene of the battle and could not see too much from his position on the plain because of the smoke*).

Lord Cardigan was not called upon to refute the suggestions because Colonel Calthorpe had partially shifted his ground; however, there was a mass of evidence against his lordship, from Lord Lucan down to private soldiers who were eye witnesses. Cardigan did, of course, have counter declarations and affidavits by other eye witnesses present at the battle. At the conclusion of the court action, his action failed, although the bench made it plain that it was only his competence being questioned and not his courage. The bench found that he had led his men to the enemy guns with valour conspicuously displayed, but thereafter his conduct as a general was open to criticism. It is fair to say that although Cardigan displayed a want of competence after the charge, he had only lost contact with his men through his brave persistence in galloping too far ahead of them!

Return home

The newspaper accounts of the charge of the Light Brigade received wide circulation in England by the time Cardigan's ship berthed at Folkestone on 13th January 1855. The town offered him a rapturous welcome, and in London he was mobbed by enthusiastic crowds. On 16th January, at Queen Victoria's invitation, he was received at Windsor to explain to her and Prince Albert details of the battle, to which the Queen noted how modestly he presented the story. But it was with a lack of reticence that he behaved during future public appearances. On 5th February he gave a highly exaggerated account of his participation in the charge at a banquet held in his honour at the Mansion House in London. A few days later, on 8th February, he made a speech in his home town of Northampton.

This is where he described how he had shared some of the privations of his men by living the whole time in a common tent, and how, after the charge, he rallied his troops and pursued fleeing enemy artillerymen as far as the Tchernaya River – none of which we know were true. Lord Cardigan was now made inspector-general of cavalry, and although the government recommended him for the Order of the Garter, Her Majesty the Queen denied him this because of previous unseemly incidents in his private life – instead he was invested as a knight in the Order of the Bath.

Despite the Queen's reservations, Lord Cardigan was made colonel of the 5th Dragoon Guards in 1859, but formally retired in 1860 – this included promotion to lieutenant general of course, and he at last became colonel of his favourite regiment, the 11th Hussars, which he had first commanded way back in 1836! Her Majesty the Queen, however, blocked his colonelcy of one of the household regiments because of an affair whilst still married to his wife, Elizabeth. Lord Cardigan's last military function was a mounted review of the 11th Hussars before their embarkation for India in May of 1866.

After his retirement, Lord Cardigan lived happily at Deene Park near Corby, Northamptonshire, which was his ancestral family home. He enjoyed horse racing, hunting and shooting. He was also a keen yachtsman, and often attended Cowes week every year, obtaining the rank as a commodore of the Royal Southern Yacht Club. Lord Cardigan died from injuries received by a fall from his horse on 28th March 1868, possibly caused by a stroke. He was buried in the family vaults at St Peter's Church, Deene.

St Peter's Church

Deene Park

15. QUESTIONS

Now we have examined most of the Crimean war, from the arrival of the allied forces at Calamita Bay, the battle of the Alma, the siege of Sevastopol, the battle of Balaclava including the charge of the Light Brigade, Inkerman and the eventual outcome of hostilities. Of course, I could have written much more detail of the various events and ended up with a thick volume similar to the many written already; so how do these volumes differ from those that have gone before? There are several things: firstly, where possible, I have included photographs or portraits of all the men involved so that you, the reader, can see what those men looked like – the men who were responsible for what occurred, and the deaths of many good soldiers in the Crimea. Secondly, I have included where possible aerial shots or maps of the ground over which events happened, so that perhaps the reader can imagine themselves being on a horse of a regiment as it lined up uneasily for the charge of the Light Brigade. (*Courtesy of Google Earth for most of these*)

Your own personal charge

What were those men thinking when Lord Cardigan gave the word of command to advance, and what was that terrifying scream after just a few moments at the trot, followed by the sound of the first shells whistling close by? Did you see Captain Nolan's chest explode as he took the brunt of the impact and his horse charged back in the opposite direction towards you, causing your neighbours horse to collide with yours, crushing your leg painfully? The sound of the cannon on the hills to your left and right come closer and closer until you see direct hits ahead, with men and horses falling painfully – are they getting up again and dusting down, or remounting and trying to catch up with the rest?

Now your horse begins to snort as you come to an uncontrolled gallop, with men shouting, shrieking and jeering so you have to join in, your arm aching from carrying your sword and the other from grasping the reins for dear life – the cannon in front are deafening, smoking, and surely the boss isn't charging directly into them? Is he insane? You guide your terrified horse towards a big gap between the Russian guns, just like your fellow riders who have also managed to keep upright in the saddle. They're ahead of you, bewildered just like you as you squeeze behind them and with no control can only cling to your horse and hope it ends in a moment.

But it doesn't, for the colonel is screaming for you to follow him and you do, pulling up rapidly with the others as you come up against mounted enemy cavalry and charging Russian infantry screaming like banshees. The noise, smoke and dust is overwhelming but at least the cannon has stopped. You look ahead and see your colleagues trying to control their horses whilst slashing downwards with their swords at what can only be Russian soldiers on the ground. Everyone is swearing at the top of their voices, including the horses it seems. Your horse bangs into those of your fellow troopers and crushes your leg again and some enemy soldiers with it. At last you are free. Your sergeant is there, shouting and bellowing at everyone.

'Kill them lads! Kill them! Slash, don't stab!'

You feel a slight stabbing pain in your calf and see a spot of blood as a pointy blade withdraws – an ugly Russian soldier with rotten teeth grins at you as he tries to pull your leather boot from the stirrup whilst shouting at you in Russian – this makes you mad and stirs you into action. Your fellow troopers are there to back you up if necessary, so you slash wildly at the Russian and see cut marks on his overcoat – you can't be sure if your sword cut flesh or cloth, but within moments you're on the next man, and then the next until, after a few seconds more, you hear an English officer shouting to get back.

Nobody hesitates as you join forces and follow the leader, hoping he knows where he is going. This is so unlike the training school lessons! You slow gallop past the silent enemy guns, swinging your battered sword at crouching and cowering Russian artillery men but probably missing them all. Dust hurts your eyes, causing them to stream, and the smoke from discharged artillery shells burns your nose and throat. Someone rides alongside you; it is your young officer, minus helmet and with blood streaming from a gash behind his ear. His uniform is mostly torn to shreds.

'Come on trooper, increase your speed!' he shouts.

But your horse can only make a medium trot and no more. The hill is slowing you down. Other horses swirl in the dust on your right – you can barely make them out, but they are Russians! Your young officer holds a pistol and fires at them – one man falls in the dirt, writhing, but you both ride on until your officer's horse collapses. You slow down and reach down a bloodied hand – yes, you've been injured there too, but feel no pain. You haul your officer on to the back of your horse and move away at a steady trot. The dust clears now and you see the way ahead.

A line of colourful horses bars the way – part of the Heavy Brigade! Thank the lord! Your own survivors gather just to the right of them, the men swearing and gulping water from their flasks. The Heavy Brigade cheers as each survivor reaches safety; they cheer at you. On a small rise in the ground to your left you notice a dozen men gathered, mostly wearing cocked hats – it is the senior staff, Lord Cardigan is amongst them and probably Lords Lucan and Raglan too. Voices there are raised – you want to ride over and give them the sharp end of your tongue, but you can't. Others do, however – Lord Paget bravest amongst them.

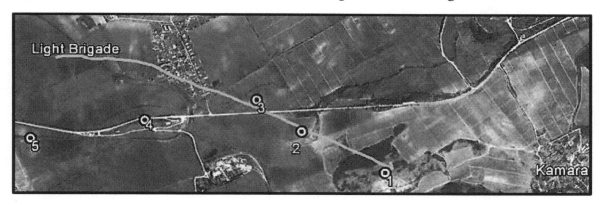

Correct interpretation of the 4th order?

Serious questions

Perhaps it could have been like that? In trying to clear Lord Cardigan of blame for the disaster, a number of fundamental questions need to be answered as best possible, and these I discuss next. **What could have happened had Lord Cardigan and his brigade gone to the correct destination, and stopped captured British guns being moved by Russians?** We can never really know but only speculate. Whilst advancing, the brigade would not be under artillery fire from the enemy, since the Russians would not be firing on their own men occupying Redoubts 3 – 1.

Neither could they turn the captured British guns on the brigade. The likelihood was that the Russians would flee the redoubts, like the Turks had earlier that morning. Lord Raglan's 4th order would have been fulfilled, and the redoubts once more be in allied hands. The nearest Russian guns were at Kamara, at a range of about 1400 yards, and the Causeway Heights would make the Russians think again if they tried to attack Balaclava via that route.

Why did Sir Cathcart prefer to eat breakfast, rather than send down his 4th Division as ordered by Lord Raglan? Again this can only be speculation. Cathcart's men had just come off night duty at Sevastopol, and it would only be fair to assume the general wanted them to have breakfast first before resting. He himself insisted on breakfast first when the messenger from Lord Raglan arrived at his tent. If we remember, Sir Cathcart was stationed close to The Col and was to assist Sir Colin Campbell and his 93rd Sutherland Highlanders (see volume II). He was dressed and in his tent when the staff officer arrived. The gist of the conversation is that the officer told Sir George that Lord Raglan requests he move his division immediately to the assistance of the Turks.

The divisional commander, of course, said that it was quite impossible, and when the startled staff officer replied that his orders were very positive and that the Russians were advancing upon Balaclava, Sir Cathcart replied that he couldn't help that, and that the greater portion of his men had only just come in from the trenches. Sir George then told the staff officer that if he would not sit down in his tent for breakfast, then he may as well go back to Lord Raglan and tell him 4th Division could not move.

Sir George finally said that he would consult with his own staff officers as to whether anything could be done, and a short time later, bugles sounded and the division marched away. Now, we may consider Sir George to be an obstinate old man; one who refused to change his behavior and was difficult to deal with, and yet he had a gentler side to his character too. When one of his ADC's was sick (Colonel Gilbert Elliot), Sir George wrapped him up in a blanket and saw him off to Balaclava to recuperate. Thus the fortunate Elliot missed the battle of Inkerman, where his boss Sir George was killed leading the division.

The kindly Sir George revealed to Elliot, as they cruised to the Crimea, that in his jacket pocket he had a document enabling him to take over command of the army in the event of Lord Raglan's death. He did not like the arrangement, but only took it at the request of the Queen. Sir George had then told Elliot that, in the event of his death, he was to retrieve the document and take it to Lord Raglan. As it happened, Sir George gave up the document to Lord Raglan two weeks before he died at Inkerman, and Sir James Simpson was to take over in the event of Lord Raglan's death.

Why did Lord Cardigan not follow up the opportunity to attack the fleeing Russian cavalry following their defeat by the Heavy Brigade? This vexing question has been discussed many times; Lord Cardigan's recollection of events was that he had been ordered into a particular position by Lucan, his superior officer, with orders on no account to leave it and to defend it against any Russian attack – the enemy did not approach his position, however. Lucan's recollection of events was that he told Cardigan he was going to leave him and that he (Cardigan) should remember that he had been put in that position by Lord Raglan for the defence of it.

Lucan's orders to Cardigan were that he was to attack anything and everything that shall come within his reach, but to be careful of columns (*cavalry*) or squares (*infantry*), though neither came within reach (*they were about 1000 yards away*). So, Cardigan remained where he was. Which man was right? Commander of 17th Lancers, Captain William Morris, realized this opportunity and swears he approached Lord Cardigan and pleaded that the opportunity was too good to miss, but that the commander of the Light Brigade refused to move.

Lord Cardigan in an affidavit, says that Captain Morris never gave him any advice nor made any proposal of the sort; it was not his duty to do so and that he did not commit any such irregularity. However, Somerset Calthorpe, Lord Raglan's aide who was also present, confirms Morris' statement, as did James Wightman. If Morris, Calthorpe and Wightman confirm this, then Lord Cardigan can be either lying in his affidavit, or his memory was mistaken. Nevertheless, the opportunity was lost forever and the Russian cavalry, fresh from defeat at the hands of the Heavy Brigade, was able to regroup at the far end of the north valley in preparation for what was to come next.

Was there really a conflict of orders?

The very question: were those senior men on the ground confused by that infamous 4th order from Lord Raglan? Lord Lucan's reason was disclosed in a speech he gave to the House of Lords on 19th March 1855. Lucan's first note was that no infantry had, at this time, arrived from Sevastopol. He therefore remained between his two brigades, anxiously waiting their arrival on the plain. When the infantry finally did arrive, instead of being formed for an attack or to support, they were for the greater part sitting or lying down with their arms piled. Between thirty to forty minutes had elapsed and the whole infantry had not arrived. Then Captain Nolan galloped up with the 4th order; in Lord Lucan's opinion, it was a fresh order, quite independent of any previous order and having no connection with the 3rd order, or indeed any other order.

Lord Lucan positively affirmed that neither Lord Raglan or General Airey, or by any other person whatsoever, did he ever hear or suppose that any connection existed or intended to exist, between this new order and the preceding one. Lucan then thought it time to show those lords gathered what an aide-de-camp actually is, and he referred to page 59 of Queen's Regulations. 'All orders sent by aides-de-camp are to be delivered in the plainest terms, and are to be obeyed with the same readiness as if delivered personally by the general officers to whom such aides-de-camp are attached.'

Is not therefore an aide-de-camp the organ of his general, he stated? And whether a general officer who took upon himself to disobey an order brought by an aide-de-camp, verbal or written, would not risk the loss of his commission? If this were not so, why could not an orderly dragoon convey orders as well as an aide-de-camp? An aide-de-camp is chosen because he is an officer of education and intelligence, he is, therefore, supposed to deliver an order more correctly, and is considered as being in the confidence of his general.

Was not then Captain Nolan in General Airey's confidence? Originally the order had been given to Captain Nolan verbally and it was only when that officer turned his horse away that Airey detained him and committed the instructions to writing. Lord Lucan then asked any reasonable man, after this, whether any mistake was or could have been committed by Captain Nolan. And how could Lucan at that time, doubt but that Captain Nolan had been instructed to deliver to him the positive order to attack which he did?

Lucan next directed their lordships attention to the 4th order. In the order it states '*French cavalry is on your left,*' evidently for the purpose of informing him where the French cavalry were; an admission that they were out of his sight, if not out of reach, and again informing Lucan that it was a combined movement in which they were to join and assist him. His lordship felt, ordered as he was to advance immediately without an opportunity of sending to ask for further instructions, that he could not fail to perform his part of this combined movement and so leave the brunt of the affair to be borne by the French cavalry alone.

Under these circumstances, his course was clear; he considered it a positive duty to order Lord Cardigan to advance with the light cavalry brigade and to lead the heavy cavalry brigade to its support. In the evening of the action, Lord Lucan continued, he saw Lord Raglan whose first remark to him was 'you have lost the Light Brigade.' He at once denied that he had lost them, as he had only carried out the orders conveyed to him, written and verbal, by Captain Nolan. Lord Raglan then said that Lucan was a lieutenant general; he should therefore have exercised his discretion and by not approving of the charge, should not have made it. Lord Raglan subsequently said that Lucan had not moved sufficiently in advance in the previous movement (*3rd order*).

Lord Lucan continued and stated that it was a fact that the Duke of Cambridge, commanding 1st Division, received no order to give the cavalry any support; nor did Sir George Cathcart of 4th Division. Lord Lucan thus placed his division in the position which Lord Raglan's aide-de-camp (*Nolan*) told him to take, and there waited for the co-operation of the infantry, but that was never given. From thirty to forty minutes' time elapsed between the receipt of the 3rd and 4th orders. If the former order had been badly carried out, Lord Raglan was in a position to see it and had only to send an aide to point out Lord Lucan's error.

The cavalry was ordered to advance and take advantage of any opportunity to recover the heights. Did any opportunity occur which Lucan neglected; was he to create the opportunity himself or was he to do more than to profit by the opportunities created by others? As for recovering the heights, he declared that there was not a single Russian on the heights west of Redoubt 3, for after the heavy dragoon charge in the morning (*the charge of the Heavy Brigade*), the enemy evacuated Redoubts 6, 5, and 4 – Redoubt 4 was subsequently occupied by Cathcart. If, as Lord Lucan contended, there were no Russians until Redoubt 3, and they were all either in that fort or beyond it, he would wish to ask any military man how he was to execute that 3rd order.

Was it to be supposed that Lord Raglan intended the cavalry to attack Redoubt 3, or was it not more reasonable to suppose that the infantry was to attack it, and that the cavalry was to wait for the opportunity of cutting off the retreat of the enemy when the assault proved successful? Had his lordship acted otherwise than he did, he would have been charged, and justly charged, with imprudence and incapacity! As Lord Lucan had already stated, there were no heights occupied by Russians to recover, but there were three redoubts.

He knew that it was intended the infantry should attack and retake them, and it was the wish of Sir George Cathcart to make the attempt – but it was not attempted, because it was considered that they could not be held and that it was not worth the loss of life that must necessarily attend such an assault. Lord Raglan had proceeded with 'so little had he (*Lucan*) sought to do as he had been directed that he had no men in advance of his main body.' The fact is, Lord Cardigan's brigade was so much in advance that Lord Lucan received a communication from his lordship through his aide-de-camp objecting to stand where he was, because the position was so much in advance and he expected the batteries on the left to open upon him. Lord Raglan had also said 'he (*Lucan*) made no attempt to regain the heights.' Lord Lucan has already stated that firstly, there were no heights but only redoubts to regain, and secondly, that he had not the promised co-operation of the infantry.

Lord Raglan had continued 'and was so little informed of the position of the enemy that he (*Lucan*) asked Captain Nolan what and where he was to attack, as neither enemy nor guns were in sight.' Lord Lucan was sensible of the absurdity and uselessness of the 4th order and when he (*Nolan*) persisted in his orders to attack, he replied 'attack, sir! – attack what, and where? What guns are we to recover?' Captain Nolan pointed to the farther end of the valley and said 'there, my Lord, are your guns and your enemy.' Lord Lucan had already stated the erroneous impression which prevailed that the Russians were at that moment taking away allied guns from Redoubts 1, 2 and 3, and the spot pointed at by Captain Nolan was in the direction they would have been taken.

The guns were not moved at all that day, and therefore the whole was a misconception. Lord Lucan said it was not trifling to pretend that there was no order to attack, when it was desired (*for the cavalry*) to advance rapidly to the front, to follow the enemy and to try to prevent the enemy from carrying away the guns? Ask any military man whether such an order means anything but attack? Could it be pretended that the cavalry was to advance slowly under a cross fire of batteries and having reached the enemy was not to attack them, but to halt with hands in pockets? The idea, Lord Lucan said, was too puerile and absurd.

But to proceed, he was told that in carrying out this operation, a troop of horse artillery may accompany. Lord Lucan reiterated that the word 'may' was here introduced in the 4th order. He therefore considered much of the order discretionary and did not take the troop. The artillery would have had to proceed up a long valley, much of it ploughed land, under a cross fire of batteries, and without a chance of ever bringing their guns usefully into action. He considered that he exercised a wise discretion, for had the troop of horse artillery accompanied the cavalry, the horses must have been killed and the guns lost.

Raglan's letter had proceeded with 'he was informed that the French cavalry was on the left and he did not invite their co-operation.' This is a most extraordinary charge, Lord Lucan said. They were out of sight on the other side of the ridge of the Inkerman valley and so much nearer to Lord Raglan and General Canrobert than to him. He knew not what was the force of French cavalry, how commanded or what orders they had received. Moreover, his advance was to be immediate and he could not have communicated with the French cavalry in less than a quarter of an hour.

He continued by mentioning that three squadrons of French chasseurs most gallantly attacked a Russian battery in flank and reverse (*on Fedioukine Heights*), silenced several of its guns and thus rendered the greatest service to the Heavy Brigade. [7] Was there then a conflict of orders? The orders we're talking about were Lord Raglan's 3rd and 4th orders, as we know, so were those orders conflicting enough to cause confusion between the two senior most commanders on the ground?

3rd order: 'Cavalry to advance and take advantage of any opportunity to recover the heights. They will be supported by the infantry which have been ordered. Advance on two fronts.'

4th order: 'Lord Raglan wishes the cavalry to advance rapidly to the front – follow the enemy and try to prevent the enemy carrying away the guns – troop horse artillery may accompany – French cavalry is on your left (signed R Airey) immediate.'

You don't need to be a military person to understand these two orders. In the 3rd order, the cavalry is to advance to recover the heights, supported by infantry, and to advance on two fronts. From a lieutenant general's point of view, there are but three queries: what heights, what infantry, and what two fronts? Even Lord Lucan must have known what heights the order referred too: Causeway or Fedioukine? The infantry he has already identified as being from Sir George Cathcart's 4th Division. Advance on two fronts is more difficult to define; but the short of it probably means the cavalry on one side of the Causeway Heights (north valley) with the supporting infantry on the other side (south valley) – alternatively, two fronts could mean an advance by both 1st and 4th Infantry Divisions, since they had been ordered on to the plain.

As it turned out, there was a forty-minute delay waiting for the infantry to arrive, no thanks to Sir George Cathcart insisting on eating breakfast first! When his men were in position, they did not take an immediate supporting stance but instead piled their arms as they would whilst waiting for further orders. All of this must have frustrated both Lord's Raglan and Lucan. Hence we come to the infamous 4th order. Time for Lord Raglan is now of an essence; advance rapidly to the front, follow the enemy, prevent them carrying away the British guns, horse artillery may accompany, French cavalry on the left. Immediate!

This order has many more queries to it but even Lord Lucan should have sussed it out – but the main query is the advancing rapidly to the front – the front leads directly to the Russian guns at the far end of the north valley; but not if you combine the 3rd order with the 4th and accept that the 4th order followed because the 3rd had not been acted upon, for various reasons. Recover the heights it says quite clearly. Now the order does not mention supporting infantry; it was to be solely a cavalry affair, with troop horse artillery accompanying if required, and the French cavalry on the left. But the French had no known orders to advance with Lucan's Cavalry Division.

Because of time restraints, Lucan could not wait another half an hour for queries to be clarified; he had to act alone and immediately, and here he fails and clears Lord Cardigan of any blame for what was to follow. He fails because of a lack of communication between himself and Lord Cardigan; he does not show the written order to Cardigan, who may have interpreted it differently, but instead orders him to attack the guns at the far end of the valley despite neither order having the word attack in the text. He blames Lord Raglan for demanding it.

Lord Cardigan in the lords

On the same day that Lord Lucan addressed the lords regarding his part in the disaster, Lord Cardigan also made a short speech regarding some of the allegations. He regretted immediately that he should be called upon to make any remarks, or take any part in the proceedings. He arose only to correct a statement made with respect to himself by Lord Lucan. The noble Earl, in his address to the lords, said that he (*Cardigan*) sent his aide-de-camp to the lieutenant general, to state that the force of the enemy was so numerous in the front of the Light Brigade that he felt it difficult to hold his ground. The statement of Lord Lucan was not right, as Cardigan sent no such message whatever.

In a message sent by Lord Cardigan to Lord Lucan, he said that, as he had perceived a movement was going to be made, he begged to point out the hills on both sides of the valley leading down to the valley at right angles with it, in which was the Russian battery, with the cavalry behind it – that these hills were occupied by Russian riflemen and artillery. Cardigan sent this message, and when the lieutenant general came in front and ordered him to attack the battery in the valley, behind which was placed the large force of Russian cavalry – which had been perfectly perceptible to himself and to the whole of the Light Brigade for at least twenty minutes – his reply to Lord Lucan was 'certainly sir; but before I go I must be allowed to point out that the hills on both sides of the valley leading to the battery are covered with Russian artillery and riflemen.'

The answer he received back was 'I cannot help that; they are Lord Raglan's positive orders.' This also shows that Lord Lucan believed the target to be at the far end of the north valley. Lord Cardigan immediately obeyed his orders; and so true was the report he had made with regard to the Russian artillery and riflemen. The brigade had not advanced far before Captain Nolan, who was galloping about in front at about the distance of 100 yards from the Light Brigade and in no way leading the charge, was killed by a shell from one of those flank batteries which Cardigan had pointed out. He had nothing further to say; he only wished to remove any misconception as to his having said that the Light Brigade was not safe in the position in which they were placed.

Was Captain Nolan disrespectful to Lords Lucan and Cardigan, and why did he break away from Captain Morris to ride after Cardigan?

For once here we have eye witnesses as to what is supposed to have happened. Having read the 4th order from Lord Raglan and told Nolan of the uselessness of such an attack and the dangers attending it, Nolan felt it necessary to respond on behalf of Lord Raglan. He reiterated the words of Lord Raglan for the benefit of Lord Lucan and the staff officers gathered close by: 'Lord Raglan's orders are that the cavalry should attack immediately,' to which Lord Lucan said loudly 'attack sir! Attack what? What guns, sir?' In his House of Lord's speech given later by Lord Lucan on 19th March 1855, some historians have him changing this to the words 'where and what to do?' However, I cannot find this in Hansard. Captain Nolan may have perceived the same as Lord Raglan from the Sapoune Heights, with Russians trying to remove the captured allied guns on Redoubts 1 – 3.

Down on the plain, however, the enemy could not be seen doing this, and the only guns then clearly visible were those at the far end of the valley (*and perhaps some of those on the Fedioukine Heights, since Lord Cardigan noticed them*). No other aide-de-camp would speak with such disrespect to a high ranking officer such as Lord Lucan as Captain Nolan – but perhaps it was not really disrespect, but an eager longing for Lucan to speed things along before the enemy succeeded in removing the captured allied guns.

Certainly Lord Lucan felt that the captain was talking to him in a disrespectful manner, but then Nolan was an ADC representing Lord Raglan; whatever Nolan said was technically the wishes of the commander-in-chief up on the Sapoune Heights. Nolan's words were delivered, Lord Lucan says, in a most disrespectful but significant manner, and his ADC, Captain Walker, described the delivery of the order as by an officer hostile to Lord Lucan.

Did Captain George Lockwood ride over to Sir Cathcart to hurry up some infantry support before re-joining the charge?

As we know from *Volume II*, Captain George Lockwood was Lord Cardigan's aide-de-camp and part of the staff riding just behind his lordship during the charge – along with Lieutenant Maxse and Sir George Wombwell. Sir George Cathcart and 4th Division was very slow in obeying Lord Raglan's order that they was to assist the Turks (*later changed by the aide delivering the message to assisting Sir Colin Campbell's 93rd Sutherland Highlanders).* So slow, in fact, that Richard Airey put in an appearance and took control of the HQ staff. 'Sir George Cathcart,' Airey said, 'Lord Raglan wishes you to advance immediately and recapture the redoubts.'

He then turned to one of the staff officers present and said 'you are acquainted with the position of each redoubt; remain with Sir George Cathcart and show him where they are.' 4th Division continued on to the open plain, moving east and passing empty Redoubts 6 and 5, where they left some men to man them before marching towards Redoubt 4. At empty Redoubt 4, the men lay down as the accompanying artillery opened fire on Redoubt 3 (the Arabtabia), which was occupied then by Russian troops from Odessa Regiment; but no further attempt was made to recapture Redoubts 3, 2 and 1 by Sir George Cathcart. It is believed by some that Lord Cardigan sent back his ADC Lockwood just before the charge, to ascertain if infantry was going to support the Light Brigade. Why would Cardigan do this?

Casting our minds back to Lord Raglan's third order of that day to Lord Lucan, there was the promise of infantry support: '*Cavalry to advance and take advantage of any opportunity to recover the heights. They will be supported by the infantry which have been ordered. Advance on two fronts.*' Lord Cardigan later denied that he sent Captain Lockwood on such a task, and this might be supported by Lieutenant Henry Maxse, who made a statement saying that Captain Lockwood was with him throughout the whole of the charge. If such a move was made by Lockwood, then the nearest British infantry battalions were those of Sir George Cathcart's 4th Division stationed at Redoubt 4 some 500 yards or so away from the brigade.

The absence of the infantry on the scene, and Lord Lucan permitting the cavalry to begin a charge without infantry support, is one of the many controversies surrounding the charge. As the Light Brigade began its advance down the valley, Captain Lockwood was probably performing some duty which separated him from the other staff; there was an idea that he rode to the ground where some of the infantry battalions were halted (Redoubt 4), addressed a general whom he found there (*Sir George Cathcart*), announced that the Light Brigade were about to engage in some ugly task and urged that it should be supported by infantry.

According to Henry Maxse [8] this supposition is incorrect. Captain Lockwood started in front of the Light Brigade from the moment of its advance, about four horse lengths to the left and some five or six lengths to the right rear of Lord Cardigan. Henry Maxse reports a loud ringing cheer and remembers the gallant bearing of Lockwood as he turned in his saddle about three-quarters of the way down would never be effaced from Maxse's memory, and doubtless in the recollection of others. That was the last time Maxse saw Lockwood; he was not near him on passing the Russian batteries at the end of the charge. Maxse also took the opportunity in writing to *The Times* of stating his impression that Captain Nolan intended to charge the same guns attacked (*at the far end of the north valley*) and no other.

Maxse also had no recollection of Nolan's divergence in the manner described by others such as Alexander Kinglake, either by deed or gesture, until after he was struck down; then his horse took the line pointed out. Although not highly relevant to the charge of the Light Brigade, Henry Maxse's letter to the newspaper in 1868 shows that his late colleague George Lockwood was present throughout the charge of the Light Brigade, until killed just before reaching the Russian guns. His evidence is also supported by Lord Cardigan, who also denied sending his senior ADC to hurry the infantry.

Why did the French cavalry not join in the charge, as written in Lord Raglan's 4th order, but instead mounted the Fedioukine Heights?

Would French assistance have helped the Light Brigade if they accompanied them during the charge? Probably the outcome would have been higher casualties than those just suffered by the British alone. The 4th Regiment of Chasseurs d'Afrique cleared the Fedioukine Heights of two Russian half batteries of artillery (8 guns in total – 4 of which the Russians managed to tow away safely), two Russian infantry battalions, and some Black Sea Cossacks, ensuring the Light Brigade would not be hit by fire from that left flank, and later providing cover for the surviving elements of the brigade as they withdrew. The French suffered 38 casualties (*10 killed*) that morning. General d'Allonville was the brigade commander with 4th Chasseurs d'Afrique, commanded by Colonel Coste de Champeron.

General Morris saw instantly the route taken by the Light Brigade along the north valley, and the terrible error unfolding, so he decided immediately to support them by attacking the enemy forces nearest him – those were Jabrokritsky and his guns on the Fedioukine Heights. Since Lord Lucan had already started off after Cardigan with the Heavy Brigade, there was no time to confer. General d'Allonville was given his orders to ascend the Fedioukine Heights and 4th Chasseurs d'Afrique moved off. At the head of the attack force were two squadrons commanded by Major Abdelal, with the other two squadrons commanded by Colonel Champeron. His force inclined to the left on top of the heights and attacked the two foot battalions supporting the enemy guns.

Major Abdelal attacked the actual guns, only to find half of them being limbered up by the Russians and moved away to safety. The Russian infantry support did not wait for the French to arrive, but quickly fled; likewise did the Black Sea Cossacks. Not all Russians fled the heights though; General Jabrokritsky led two foot battalions of the Vladimir Regiment to attack the French – there was little in the way of fighting by this stage as General Morris sounded the recall for his French forces. At least the removal of the guns by the Russians gave time for the retreating survivors of the Light Brigade to seek sanctuary. Whether Lord Lucan mentioned to Lord Cardigan that the French cavalry was available on the left I cannot say with any certainty. The 4th order mentions them for Lord Lucan, but the instant Cardigan advanced Lucan had to follow with two regiments of the Heavy Brigade. There was no time for him to confer with General Morris for use of the Chasseurs d'Afrique.

Where was the brigade commander during the fight with the Russians, who saw him on the battlefield, and was it his duty to stay and direct his brigade, fight the enemy on his own, or preserve his life for future duty?

Nobody saw Lord Cardigan during the melee at the guns or during the retreat. Those immediately following him, his three aide-de-camps Lockwood, Wombwell and Maxse, had all been disabled (*Lockwood was killed*) but there was also likely the standard bearer and trumpeter too. In the confusion of deafening noise and choking smoke, all seem to have lost contact with his lordship. Next, Cardigan cleared the dense smoke and found himself facing some retreating Russian cavalry, who fronted. A Russian officer from the house of Prince Radzivill was amongst them, and recognized Lord Cardigan from a previous visit to England in happier times. He ordered the Cossacks to bring him in unhurt, by way of a bribe, and two men tried with their lances to do so, but Lord Cardigan refused to surrender despite receiving a slight hip wound.

One of the Cossack lances became entangled with his lordships gold pelisse (*short fur lined jacket usually worn hanging loose over the left shoulder of hussar light cavalry soldiers, to prevent sword cuts*), almost throwing from him the saddle of his horse. Lord Cardigan thought it better to retreat from the scene, which he promptly did, finding himself alone near the silent Russian guns again. During the charge itself, Captain Morris described Lord Cardigan's manner as 'nothing could be better. He put himself just where he ought, about in front of my right squadron, and went down in capital style.'

He had led the brigade quietly, just as it ought to be, in short like a gentleman. [9] At the guns, Lord Cardigan saw the backs of men from 13th Light Dragoons and 17th Lancers retreating in groups up the valley. Although he thought these men were the remains of his front line, he was in fact mistaken, for these were disabled and wounded men, or men whose horses were wounded and could go no further. What he did not see was the rest of the brigade still fighting towards the aqueduct on the left flank, nor the remains of Shewell's regiment fighting on the right flank towards the centre.

Lord Cardigan then satisfied himself that there was nothing useful he could do without first following their retreat; his supports (4th, 8th, 11th) were nowhere to be seen either, and his primary duty was to the first line (17th, 13th) who appeared to be retreating. He so decided to follow the retreating first line without issuing further orders or rallying his men. Many historians believe he should have gone quickly to find Lucan or Scarlett and sought help to extricate the remains of his brigade from the enemy. He may have believed that no reinforcement could save them from destruction – although he had no regard for his own personal safety during the charge, he appears during the retreat to have cared for himself and all but forgotten his brigade.

It struck him during the walk back that it would be inconsistent from what is usual or expected from a general to retreat in such an isolated position, alone, therefore he moved slowly when clear of the Russian lancers who were trying to spring a trap on the remainder of the brigade. Eventually, he arrived back at the spot occupied by General Scarlett. His first words, as we may well imagine, was to run out against Captain Nolan. He was stopped when General Scarlett pointed out he had nearly ridden over Nolan's dead body (*it is not clear whether it was Scarlett who had nearly ridden over Nolan's dead body and was telling Cardigan, or Cardigan himself*). Lord Cardigan then resumed walking back to the area his brigade had been prior to the off.

General Scarlett swears that Lord Lucan was present when this conversation took place; Lucan says he was not present and saw Cardigan when everything was over. It seems, according to Lucan, that Cardigan rode past him at a distance of about 200 yards. I think we must conclude that Lord Cardigan did lead his brigade beyond the Russian guns during the attack; that Lord Lucan did not brief him properly as to the additional help available (*troop horse artillery and the 4th Chasseurs d'Afrique*), and that he suddenly found himself cut off by Cossacks. One Cossack officer recognized him and ordered him captured unhurt, but the Cossacks did injure him with their lances, after which he sensibly withdrew.

Back at the guns, he saw through the dust and smoke only his first line retreating, and no signs of his supports; that he concluded there was nothing more useful he could do since his retreating men were in groups and appeared injured. And so he decided retreat was the best form of action to take – he may have galloped through the Russian lancers forming on the Fedioukine flank, but thereafter he returned at a slow pace.

16. CLEARING CARDIGAN

We have now come full circle and down to the nitty gritty; clearing Cardigan. There are many detailed books on the subject of the charge, Balaclava, Sevastopol and the Crimean war. Historian's today struggle to find new facts about the charge of the Light Brigade, because it is 163 years now since it took place. Nobody has recently come forward and said 'look, here are new documents pertaining to the charge!' If only! Today, we do have a few letters, transcripts from the House of Lords and fine works such as Kinglake's volumes written shortly after the battle. But even these cannot be taken as gospel, although Kinglake tries where possible to quote his sources – his sequencing of events goes array at times. What is different about these works (and that of my series *Clearing Reno* and the battle of the Little Bighorn), is that an accumulation of author's works can be compared, and where they quote the same source details, assume them to be correct.

It is unfortunate that there was no proper inquiry into the charge, unlike that of the battle of the Little Bighorn (Marcus Reno's inquiry of 1879). Also, it is possible today to correlate the rough maps and sketches drawn shortly after the charge (very much like those drawn after the battle of the Little Bighorn), with real life shots of the actual locations today. So, the magnitude of what really happened in both battles can be appreciated by the reader. The lay of the land, and height of hills etc., can now be accurately made and compared with witness statements.

Of course, the land would change over time and not look quite the same today as it did back then. These volumes about Lord Cardigan (and those of Major Marcus Reno) are entirely my own appreciation of the battles as I understand them today. The maps with their icons are also my own interpretations of the locations of things, and can only really be approximations of events; likewise, the freely available photographs of the participants – where I could match them to a name, depended on somebody else getting the name with the picture correct in the first instance! Many photographs date back 163 years, remember.

So was Lord Lucan to blame for the tragedy?

Who was really to blame for the disaster that befell the Light Brigade? This is that all important question, but perhaps we should not be trying to apportion blame because, like an air crash, usually there is a sequence of events leading to a disaster and not just one thing. My conclusions are at the end of this final chapter, but I will first go through various participants to prove or disprove their gullibility, beginning with Lord Lucan.

●Was he to blame? Well, not entirely, although his attitude left a lot to be desired; he blames many people except himself – I suppose it is only natural that he would want to clear his name, although it is quite obvious that those above him in rank laid the blame squarely upon him. Lucan cannot accept criticism of himself. Interestingly, Lord Lucan realized almost immediately, as the Light Brigade began its advance, that he might be blamed entirely for the unfolding tragedy – remember, he hands the original 4th order received from Captain Nolan to his Turkish interpreter, Sir John Blunt, for safe keeping.

●Why did he not bring the horse artillery to the Light Brigade? As we may recall early in volume II, the horse artillery, assuming it is the same that Lord Raglan refers to in the text of his 4th order, had been in action near Redoubts 3 and 4. Their commander, Captain George Maude, was seriously injured and Captain Shakespeare took them out of action because they were low on ammunition. Their withdrawal was done on Lord Lucan's orders, after he became aware of Maude's wounds – the usual wagons following with ammunition had not, for some reason, gone with the artillery to the Causeway Heights that morning.

George Maude   *d'Allonville*   *Henry Maxse*

●Why did Lord Lucan not bring the French cavalry, waiting at the rear left of the Light Brigade, into action as a support? General Morris, commander of the French cavalry division, had not long before been present on the Sapoune Heights with Lord Raglan and French commander-in-chief Canrobert. Now he joined the brigade, where General d'Allonville waited at the head of Colonel Coste de Champeron's 4th Chasseurs d'Afrique. The French cavalry command expected at any moment the Light Brigade would veer right the 30° or so needed to ascend the Causeway Heights and attack Redoubt 3.

But the Light Brigade just kept going into the narrowing jaws of hell, and so General Morris next resolved to venture French support for Lord Cardigan's attack. Silencing the enemy guns on the heights was the best possible course of action. Lord Lucan appeared to be on the right of the valley, with the Heavy Brigade and moving slowly, which left only those guns to silence on the Fedioukine Heights, from whose murderous fire Captain Nolan had been killed a few minutes before.

● Did Lord Lucan offer support to Lord Cardigan with the Heavy Brigade? Did he even suggest supporting to his lordship, like George Custer had said to Major Reno just before the battle of the Little Bighorn? I'm not seeing any evidence that Lucan told Cardigan that he would support him. In any event, Lord Lucan only advanced part way along the valley with just two of five Heavy Brigade regiments available. I can only judge that the remaining regiments of Scarlett's Brigade were in such disarray, or just too exhausted, after their own charge an hour earlier.

● Why then did Lord Lucan stop and turn about? Possibly, it had something to do with enemy cones of fire; artillery has a cone of fire through which charging enemy may get hit during its time within that cone. The cone is pretty static, since the guns do not move, other than rocking back and forth when they fire. The **first artillery cone** was up on the western Fedioukine Heights; these were the same guns that the French Chasseurs d'Afrique were about to charge and silence. The range of the cone (which widens farther away from the nozzle of the gun) depends upon the gun's poundage and elevation. The first artillery cone just about reached Redoubt 4, which stood opposite and across the north valley.

The cone was about 1300 yards wide at its maximum extent, with a length of around 1500 yards. The Light Brigade would have taken approximately 3 to 4 minutes to cross cone one at a fast trot. Considering that the Russians were not under pressure at that moment from Chasseurs d'Afrique, they could have gotten off about 70 rounds, including the fatal shot that killed Captain Nolan. The Russians had between 8 and 10 guns on the Fedioukine Heights at that time.

The **second artillery cone** met by the Light Brigade was from the actual guns standing part way across the far end of the north valley; the very target guns of the Light Brigade attack. This cone was about 2400 yards long, with a maximum width of around 500 yards at its furthest extent – the Light Brigade entered it immediately upon exiting the first cone, and remained within it until reaching their target at the end of their charge. The Russian artillery of the second cone numbered between 8 and 12 guns; the British claim 12 whereas the Russians claim 8 – in the 4 minutes or so it would have taken the Light Brigade to traverse the second cone to the actual guns themselves, the Russians could have let loose about 88 rounds. The effects, although devastating to the men and horses hit, was not as bad when fired face on (as opposed to enfilade fire, in other words, side on fire along the longitudinal axis of the charging cavalry). The men could usually see cannon balls coming towards them and swerve aside as the ball bounced two or three times before rolling to a halt on the ground.

The **third artillery cone** met by the Light Brigade was perhaps the most dangerous and serious of the three; these being the Russian guns stationed around captured Redoubt 3 and whose extent crossed that of the second cone, thus leaving a large rectangular area where the brigade faced not only second cone fire from the front, but also third cone fire enfilade from the side. This enfilade came from Captain Bojanov's 7th light battery, 12th artillery brigade. He commanded 6 guns and 2 howitzers (the latter fire missiles only, instead of cannon balls or grape shot). He had just two minutes to take a pot-shot at the charging Light Brigade, during which he and his men loosed off about 32 rounds at their enemy.

• How far down the north valley did Lord Lucan ride before stopping? He had waited initially with his staff and the Heavy Brigade near Redoubt 5, and was just about parallel to the Light Brigade as it began to advance. Lord Raglan's 4th order explicitly stated that the cavalry was to advance – therefore, not just the Light Brigade, but also the Heavy Brigade, so the manoeuvre was really a divisional one. Lord Lucan, from a technical point, should have led the division from the front, but instead gave the lead to Lord Cardigan.

He left the Redoubt 5 area, leading two regiments of the heavies and within a minute, despite clinging close to the Causeway Heights, was within the first artillery cone of fire from the Fedioukine Heights. He began to take casualties during his transit through the cone, until clear the other side – when about 300 yards from the Russians in Redoubt 3 he stopped and turned about, passing close to Redoubt 4 which was then occupied by George Cathcart's men. The distance travelled in one direction by Lord Lucan was about 1900 yards, or about one mile.

• Did Lord Lucan misunderstand Raglan's orders? For this to be answered we need to understand his lordships situation at the time when Captain Nolan turned up carrying the infamous 4th order. Lord Lucan was still in 3rd order frame of mind. '*Cavalry to advance and take advantage of any opportunity to recover the heights. They will be supported by the infantry which have been ordered. Advance on two fronts.*' Lord Lucan was impatiently waiting for several things to happen to execute his 3rd order: firstly, for support of the promised infantry that had been ordered to put in an appearance, and secondly, for any opportunity to arise to recover the heights.

At about the time Captain Nolan rode out, the promised infantry had started to arrive from the Sapoune Heights near The Col; first, Cambridge's 1st Division began to deploy along the width of the south valley approximately in line with Redoubt 6. And second, George Cathcart's sleepy 4th Division (remember they had just come off night duty in the trenches) started to deploy cautiously along a line from Redoubt 6 to Redoubt 4.

As Cathcart began to deploy, Nolan arrived and handed Lucan the 4th order, hastily written by Richard Airey; as was custom before taking it, Nolan had read the scrawl to be sure he understood its contents, just in case Lord Lucan didn't. As he was about to leave, Lord Raglan called after Nolan 'tell Lord Lucan the cavalry is to attack immediately.' Here we have a serious juxtaposition between Raglan's 4th order, and his last words to Captain Nolan: '*Lord Raglan wishes the cavalry to advance rapidly to the front – follow the enemy and try to prevent the enemy carrying away the guns – troop horse artillery may accompany – French cavalry is on your left (signed R Airey) immediate,*' and to Nolan: '*tell Lord Lucan the cavalry is to attack immediately.*'

Here, we hear Lord Raglan mention the word 'attack'. This word must have been exactly what Nolan wanted to hear; for 41 days or thereabouts, the allied armies had marched, battled and sieged their way to Sevastopol. And yet the cavalry had not really done anything, nor charged, but this was, at last, their opportunity. Attack they would, now that the supreme commander-in-chief had said so. Lord Lucan took the message and read it before turning to Trumpet-Major Joy and saying 'mount the division.' Until now, for nearly an hour, he had been waiting for Cathcart's men to get into position, and now he was being told to advance rapidly to the front.

Further, from his position he could see no guns being carried away by the enemy; he was being asked to advance rapidly the cavalry (as a division) to the front, yet the Light Brigade was in the north valley and most of the Heavy Brigade was in the south valley. And what of the infantry? The new order did not say anything about them, and how could the cavalry prevent the guns being carried away without infantry support? Then there was the question of the French; the French cavalry was on the left – that was just a statement. They were gathering about 1900 yards away – just over a mile off – was he expected to ride over and give them orders, or find out their intentions?

There were few witnesses to any discussion between Lord Lucan and Captain Nolan; according to John Blunt, the civilian interpreter, it was the start of a discussion and not an argument between the two men. That was, until Nolan cut his lordship short with startling abruptness, saying 'Lord Raglan's orders are that the cavalry are to attack immediately.' He also added the words 'the guns' because Lord Lucan's angry response was 'attack sir! Attack what? What guns?'

Nolan's response is known to all; he flung out an arm, pointing not down the Causeway Heights, but down the north valley, followed by the words 'there my lord is your enemy, there are your guns.' It was about now that one of Cardigan's ADC's arrived to find out why the brigade had been ordered to mount. Who it was is not listed, but I believe it was either Lieutenant George Lockwood, or Captain Henry Maxse, since many historians think either may have been sent to inquire after Cathcart, or Lucan, for sounding the mount.

Lucan told Cardigan's ADC that the Light Brigade was to attack down the north valley. The aide raised the obvious dangers pertaining to such a manoeuvre, but Lucan simply waved him aside. Captain Walker, Lucan's ADC, was also present, along with John Blunt, when these events occurred, and was able to confirm them in letters sent home a few days after the charge – Walker confirmed that Lucan did not exercise his own judgement in carrying out the order, but asked Captain Nolan what he was to attack. [10]

Nolan, according to Walker, was personally hostile to Lucan. His lordship should have now used his discretion, as a lieutenant general, to query or change the order so that it could be carried out – as most commentators say, it was his duty to do so. It was the assumed authority of Nolan, acting for Lord Raglan, which Lucan appears to have accepted as inevitable. Nevertheless, he did challenge Nolan for the correct destination for the advance.

There was no hiding the fact that the only guns they could all see were at the far end of the north valley (and a few newly arrived guns just then being set up by Russians on the Fedioukine Heights). There can be little doubt that Lord Lucan and the staff around him, fully understood the gun target to be at the end of the north valley, and not those hidden from sight on the Causeway Heights.

Was Louis Nolan to blame for the tragedy?

Here we have the problem that the captain was killed just moments after the Light Brigade started its advance. He cannot give his side of things, but the various aides to the leading men involved can, and since this was from the mouth of Louis Nolan, cannot be deemed simple hearsay. Captain Arthur Tremayne of 13th Light Dragoons said there was no doubt that Nolan gave the order to go where they did go – but Tremayne only heard this from Lord Cardigan, who told him it repeatedly after the battle.

This then is hearsay and should not be counted upon – but with other evidence, could be deemed circumstantial; in other words, if other separate witnesses state more or less the same thing, then it is, in all probability, true. But can it be true beyond a reasonable doubt? The scene next changes from the Causeway Heights to the Balaclava north valley, where Lord Lucan and Captain Nolan rode approximately 550 yards across to Lord Cardigan at the head of the Light Brigade. Nolan followed because he wanted to join in the cavalry charge; possibly, he also wanted to be sure the order was correctly communicated to the brigade commander, too.

He had pointed to the wrong guns in the presence of the divisional commander a few minutes before, by design or mistake; he must have known the true object of Lord Raglan's 4th order, because he had seen the same view of the guns from Sapoune Heights earlier, and been briefed by Raglan and Airey before he left them. What followed next between Lucan and Cardigan varies between them both: Lucan said he told Cardigan to advance in two lines and to do so very steadily and keep the men well in hand – Cardigan said he was ordered to attack the Russians in the valley three-quarters of a mile (actually about 1¼ mile) distant.

There is no direct proof that Lucan handed the written order to Cardigan, for neither man admits it to be so; and if it had been so, then surely Cardigan would have queried the guns, the troop horse artillery, and the French cavalry with Lucan? Lord Cardigan then pointed out the folly of such an attack, to which Lord Lucan replied that Lord Raglan would have it and they had no choice but to obey. After Cardigan had saluted his acceptance of the order, Captain Nolan, who was also present, made no effort known to historians to correct the misunderstanding of both these generals.

There did follow another altercation, apparently, at this moment between Cardigan and Nolan; the words are not known other than Cardigan's reply to Nolan, which was reported by Donald Serrell Thomas in his book about Cardigan to be 'by God, if I come through this alive, I'll have you courts martialled for speaking to me in this manner.' [11] Thomas makes the case for Cardigan then giving the order to advance to the field trumpeter of 17th Lancers, John Brown, whereas Cardigan had his own man, Trumpeter Whitton, waiting immediately behind him along with brigade staff officers Mayow, Maxse, Wombwell and Lockwood.

It is more probable that the sound to advance came from Whitton, which questions the validity of Donald Thomas's book. Nolan rode to William Morris commanding the 17th and asked his permission to accompany the regiment in the charge. This was granted. The brigade was also joined by a few late comers as the advance started: two Piedmont observers (from Sardinia), Major Grovone and Lieutenant Landriani, joined the front line. Also, there was butcher John Vahey of the 17th (still wearing his bloodied butcher's clothes and riding a troop horse borrowed from the heavies).

After but 100 yards or may be less, Nolan broke away from the regiment and spurred his horse; why he did this we can only speculate but not know, since Nolan was killed. Morris is said to have shouted 'that won't do Nolan. We've a long way to go and must be steady.' I cannot find the source of these words, not even in M J Trow's book *The Pocket Hercules*, which is a biography of Captain Morris. Lord Cardigan did comment on the incident, believing Nolan was trying to force the pace.

He also described Nolan's scream sounding like that of a woman, when he eventually returned to General Scarlett. He complained of Nolan, whose dead body he had just passed, for he had not looked back and seen Nolan killed until Scarlett pointed it out. One man who did see Nolan die was Coronet Sir George Wombwell, riding with the staff of Lord Cardigan; he wrote letters describing Nolan's sword dropping to the ground but his arm remaining high in the air, followed by body spasms. [12]

Private James William Wightman of 17th Lancers wrote a description of the weird shriek and awful face of Captain Nolan – Wightman believed it was the impact of the shell which killed him and caused his horse to swerve to the right, ahead of Lord Cardigan. [13] Nobody can confirm the shouts of Nolan just before he was struck and killed – according to Trow, some heard him shout 'come on,' (thus forcing the pace), whilst others heard him shout 'threes right,' (diverting the brigade to the right, away from its present course). Again, there are no sources mentioned. Captain Morris of the 17th, Nolan's friend, does not even make any comment on paper, either.

● Perhaps quite interesting in his description of the demise of Captain Nolan, and for which I support what he said, was Corporal James Ikin Nunnerley of the 17th Lancers. He wrote an article in 1890 called '*A Short Sketch of the 17th Lancers, and Life of Sergeant-Major J I Nunnerley.*' He says that Nolan rode up to the commanding officer (Morris) and said 'now Morris, for a bit of fun!' Almost as soon as he had spoken then he was shot, giving a sort of yell that sounded like 'threes right' and threw his sword arm above his head, after which his horse wheeled to the right and Nolan fell to the rear.

Part of the 17th wheeled 'threes right' and Nunnerley gave the order 'front forward,' and so brought them into line again. Nolan did not cross ahead of Lord Cardigan, but behind him. Corporal Thomas Morley, writing two years later, supports the same view that part of the 17th did wheel slightly to the right. Of course, it is possible they did this when a shell exploded among the ranks. Either way, the indications now are that Nolan was a victim of Russian fire, rather than trying to divert the Light Brigade up onto the Causeway Heights as was generally accepted until now. Henry Maxse, Lord Cardigan's ADC, wrote to *The Times* newspaper stating that he had no recollection of Nolan attempting to create a divergence by deed or gesture.

• Was Nolan to blame for the tragedy? This is one of those questions that can never be answered properly, simply because the captain was killed and cannot answer for himself. The only things we have are eye witness descriptions of the instant Nolan was stuck by the shell, and instances of Nolan's contempt for Lord's Lucan and Cardigan. What we can confirm is that up on the Causeway Heights, Nolan did point down the north valley, instead of towards the redoubts that Lord Raglan wished the cavalry to advance too. Nolan also verbally stated before witnesses that those guns at the end of the north valley were the target guns. Whether Nolan believed this to be the case, or whether he was simply mistaken or deliberately thought those guns made a better target than those captured on the redoubts, has to be simply conjecture. Nolan can be only partially to blame for pointing down the wrong valley to Lord Lucan – but not entirely to blame.

Was Lord Raglan to blame for the tragedy?

The man at the very top will often fall on his sword – but not so Lord Raglan, the allied commander-in-chief who tried to wriggle out of any blame for the disaster. From his letters, it is clear that Raglan blamed Lucan for the debacle. 'The charge arose from the misconception of an order for the advance which Lord Lucan considered obliged him to attack at all hazards,' he said in his letter to the Secretary of State in London, dated 28th October 1854. Lord Lucan must have been under some misconception of the instruction to advance – the lieutenant general (Lucan) considered that he was bound to attack at all hazards, and accordingly ordered the Earl of Cardigan to move forward with the Light Brigade.

Attack at all hazards – Victorian words meaning to attack at any cost. Lord Raglan said other things about Lord Lucan to the Secretary of State: 'I wish I could say with his Lordship, that, having decided against his conviction, to make the movement, he did all he could to render it as little perilous as possible. This indeed is far from being the case, in my Judgment.' In this statement Lord Raglan was wrong, for Lucan had removed 11th Hussars from the front line to a new second line, thus narrowing the front of the attack force. Lucan was told, Raglan said, that the troop horse artillery might accompany the cavalry, but he did not bring it up.

But of what use, during a rapid advance, would troop horse artillery make, other than to slow down the advance? And let's not forget that the troop horse artillery had been withdrawn to get more ammunition. Lord Lucan was also informed that French Cavalry was on the left; he did not invite their co-operation. At no time did the French command send anyone across to discuss with Lord Lucan their involvement in the rapid advance of the British cavalry. Lord Raglan also said that Lucan had the whole of the heavy cavalry at his disposal. Lucan mentions having brought up only two regiments in support, but he omits all other precautions, either from want of due consideration, or from the supposition that the unseen enemy was not in such great a force as he apprehended.

Notwithstanding that he was warned by Lord Cardigan after the latter had received the order to attack. Lord Lucan did have the Heavy Brigade to hand, but had not he considered just an hour earlier that the brigade had been in mortal combat with the enemy, and would need to rest before attempting a 1½ mile advance? As for the unseen enemy Raglan mentions (Russians removing the guns), Lord Lucan could not see them, only just the guns at the end of the north valley, and some on the Fedioukine Heights. And Captain Nolan was present, pointing down the north valley.

So yes, the things mentioned by Lord Raglan in his letter of the 28th October could have been done differently by Lord Lucan with hindsight – nevertheless, for mostly sound reasons he had a defence against Raglan's allegations. We must consider the wording of Lord Raglan's main relevant orders that morning to Lord Lucan, all three of them.

- *'Cavalry to take ground to the left of second line of redoubts occupied by Turks.'*

Disappointingly for Lucan, the cavalry was not to become entangled in combat until the arrival of the two divisions sent in support of the Turks and Colin Campbell. Raglan sent Captain Wetherall down with his order; it was for the cavalry division to withdraw to the left side of Redoubt 6 and the foothills of the Sapoune Heights. But reading it, you would not understand it to be so, and it was a good job Wetherall was on hand to direct Lucan in the correct procedure.

- *'Cavalry to advance and take advantage of any opportunity to recover the heights. They will be supported by the infantry which have been ordered. Advance on two fronts.'*

Lord Lucan appears to have misunderstood or ignored this order. He first mounted his division and then moved the Light Brigade across part of the north valley, before moving the tired Heavy Brigade on to the slopes of the rise (Causeway Heights near Redoubt 5), there to await arrival of the promised infantry which had not arrived. The cavalry remained at the halt for between thirty and fifty-five minutes; reports vary. Lord Lucan appears under the impression that the infantry would take the heights with the cavalry in support, whereas the order, had he read it correctly, quite clearly states that the cavalry would be supported by the infantry that had been ordered.

Lord Raglan's 'advance on two fronts' can only mean that the cavalry was to advance with the infantry, therefore Lord Lucan was correct to delay things until George Cathcart turned up in force and was ready. There was an opportunity to recover the heights, and there was little Lucan could see from his position on the plain. Raglan's 3rd order was not possible to implement, considering Lucan and George Cathcart could not see where they were to advance. There was a staff officer, if you remember from volume II, who was told by Richard Airey 'you are acquainted with the position of each redoubt; remain with Sir George Cathcart and show him where they are.' There really was no excuse for Cathcart's dithering in confronting the enemy, but Lord Raglan's authority must be in doubt if it was necessary to send Richard Airey to goad 4th Division into action.

- *'Lord Raglan wishes the cavalry to advance rapidly to the front – follow the enemy and try to prevent the enemy carrying away the guns – troop horse artillery may accompany – French cavalry is on your left (signed R Airey) immediate.'*

The infamous 4th order has been poured over enough times already, but to summarize the irregularities in it; 'advance rapidly' rather than 'attack' – contradicted by Raglan shouting after Captain Nolan 'tell Lord Lucan the cavalry is to attack immediately,' instead of 'advance immediately.' This must have stirred up Captain Nolan when he heard it. 'To prevent the enemy carrying away the guns' – only Lord Raglan could see these guns from the Sapoune Heights, not Lord Lucan down on the plain. He does not explain which guns he is referring to.

'Troop horse artillery may accompany.' For what use? Unless they are given the opportunity to take up suitable positions and bombard the enemy before the cavalry attacks – but then they had run out of ammunition hadn't they? As for French cavalry on the left, again for what use unless there was some co-ordination between the two allies. And there wasn't. Lord Raglan's orders are dubious to say the least, unclear, imprecise and open to misinterpretation. A good candidate for the cause of the disaster.

Was Richard Airey to blame for the tragedy?

On the day, General Richard Airey was issuing Lord Raglan's orders, which he scribbled down on some old paper. The written order was then handed to Lord Raglan to read, before handing over to the ADC for delivery. To ensure correct execution, the aide read the order and was then supposed to be briefed, to make sure the contents were thoroughly understood. Once carrying the message to the receiver was done, the ADC was then acting as the mouth piece of the sender, and the receiver had to obey the order. Not all officers, of course, took full notice with the expediency required; George Cathcart, for example, insisting on having his breakfast first before deploying 4th Division on the Causeway Heights is one example. I don't blame him; he and his men had been on night duty in the trenches. Is it possible Richard Airey misunderstood, or wrote out the orders incorrectly, and perhaps Lord Raglan did not read them with as much attention as he should have?

There really is no evidence of this, so we should eliminate Airey from blame; after all, Lord Raglan was responsible for checking the written orders prior to despatch. As a by line to this, in the 1968 film of the charge starring Trevor Howard, right at the very end the senior most men are squabbling over who was responsible. Lord Lucan (played by Harry Andrews), is blamed by both Cardigan (Howard) and Raglan (John Gielgud) for the disaster, until Lucan states he was just carrying out orders delivered by Captain Nolan, written in Raglan's own hand – the piece of paper is then handed to Raglan, who reads it and hands it to Richard Airey (Mark Dignam) with the words 'Airey, you have just lost the Light Brigade!' Where the director got this idea from I couldn't say – although in an earlier scene when Raglan dictates another order, Airey is already folding the paper before Raglan finishes his order – likely this is just artistic licence!

Just who was to blame for the tragedy?

I think if we knew the answer to that, there would be very few books written about the charge of the Light Brigade. But it is an enduring mystery, and always will be, similar to the battle of the Little Bighorn in 1876 or Jack the Ripper in 1888. We can only speculate and give our various theories – hence the large numbers of books available on the subject. As a new author on the subject, I can only look at the scant evidence preserved from the time of the tragedy and read other historian's works, paying particular attention to where they obtained their sources. In these four volumes, I have endeavoured to do what few other writers have done in the past, and that is provide as many photographs or paintings of the participants whose names occur time and time again, as well as modern aerial maps of event locations based on maps of old.

For many historians, it is too easy to simply accept the old maps, passed down from generation to generation, as being gospel. With my maps, I have tried to locate as closely as possible, within reason, where events happened and to mark them on the map concerned. Much of the historic past has naturally been erased and built over by the people of the Crimea where it all happened, but much still remains. Some places are still not known, very much like some places where events happened during the battle of the Little Bighorn. Such places are, for example, Lord Raglan's location on the Sapoune Heights during the charge; it can only be an approximate position from where he could see down the north valley, simply because we do not know precisely the location.

Also, much of the Woronzoff Road, many British redoubts and the defences surrounding Sevastopol, along with the position of the 'thin red line' just north of Kadikoi, are approximations. Other things are can quite clearly still be seen: the Star Fort outline, the Inkerman ruins, Tractir Bridge and the aqueduct near the river where Russians bottled up during the charge. As for Cardigan's brigade, we know a fair amount about what happened during the charge, the fight and the retreat. Don't take too much notice of some of the paintings and films about the disaster either; you should probably know quite well by now the actual real layout of the brigade, who was where, what the intervals were between regiments, and who did what during the battle.

So, who was to blame for the disaster? An accumulation of factors attributed to the Light Brigade being in the wrong place at the wrong time. Did Raglan correctly give his infamous 4th order, and did Airey write it down properly? Did Nolan, by design or misinterpretation of the order, point out the wrong guns to Lord Lucan? Why did Lucan not deploy his artillery and the French cavalry on the flank? What if George Cathcart and 4th Division deployed much sooner? All these questions have been discussed at length in this volume and volume II. The reader will have to make up their own mind. As for me, I try not to apportion blame, but only illustrate the sequence of mistakes made, any of which were part of the error making the charge and destruction of the Light Brigade.

If I had to make a choice, I should blame the man at the very top for his poor generalship where his orders were concerned; also, the lieutenant general who, presented with such a confusing order to advance, should have raised the alarm and used his authority to keep Captain Nolan in his place until clarity of orders had been received.

Clearing Lord Cardigan

In my opinion, there were few mistakes made that day by James Brudenell, 7th Earl of Cardigan. Okay, he was late arriving from his yacht after the alarm was raised, but he sensibly pointed out the folly of cavalry attacking guns to the front, contrary to all the protocols of war. He willingly rode towards almost certain death at the head of his brigade, unaware of Russian guns on the Causeway Heights at Redoubt 3, or whether he was going to be supported by the Heavy Brigade – since we are not certain he read Raglan's order at that time, we can only speculate whether he knew of the horse artillery and the French cavalry on his left. He never mentioned after them.

Arriving at the guns and passing them, he found himself facing Russian cavalry, one officer of whom recognized him and ordered he be detained; two men tried to do that and wounded him, but he sensibly withdrew to the smoking Russian guns. Now if anything he might be censured for retreating instead of staying – but at the guns, all he could see were injured or riderless men moving back the way they had just come. Should he have tried to find the rest of his brigade? Certainly, only many of them moved well beyond the guns and were squeezing the Russian cavalry towards the aqueduct. Behind him were still Russian Cossacks, too many for him to expect them to allow him through, even if he knew where his supports were, which he did not.

Shewell of the depleted 8th Hussars had veered too far to the right at the guns, and missed them entirely. Douglas of 11th Hussars had likewise missed the guns by veering too far to his left, leaving only Paget with 4th Light Dragoons to tackle the guns on the left side. Lord Cardigan was stranded in the centre, remember, with none of his staff for protection. The supports were at least 300 yards away from him, on both sides. The central line of attack, that of 17th Lancers and 13th Light Dragoons, had been decimated and the survivors, having charged through and fought gallantly to a man, could not be mustered any further since most were wounded.

The swirling Russian Lancers at both ends of the Russian gun line were preparing to snap shut a trap for any British survivors attempting to flee. Lord Cardigan chose to gallop past them until safely clear, after which he trotted back slowly to the location of the Heavy Brigade. He was the responsible brigade commander and of his 673 men who had started off, 113 were dead (16.79% of the brigade) and a massive 134 men wounded (19.91%), meaning just over one-third (36.7%) of the brigade were casualties. Only 195 mounted men were present at first roll call after the battle. Lord Cardigan had blood on his hands, but blood as a result of the defective order received and the thoughtlessness of the lieutenant general in command of the division. So Lord Cardigan carried out his duty to the end, and must be completely exonerated and cleared of any blame for the needless destruction of the Light Brigade.

End

REFERENCES

[1] – papers relating to the recall of Lord Lucan, as described by A W Kinglake, Vol V pg 422 of the appendix.

[2] – papers relating to the letter of Lord Raglan dated the 28th October 1854 to the Secretary of State in London, as described by A W Kinglake, Vol V pg 422 of the appendix.

[3] – Lord Lucan's letter of the 30th November 1854 to Lord Raglan, as described by A W Kinglake, Vol V pg 423 of the appendix.

[4] – Lord Raglan's letter to the Duke of Newcastle as described by A W Kinglake, Vol V pg 426 of the appendix.

[5] – as told to A W Kinglake by Lord Cardigan, and described in Vol V pg 405 of the appendix.

[6] – Colonel Calthorpe's affidavit in response to Lord Cardigan's affidavits from *Cardigan v Calthorpe*.

[7] – *Hansard's Parliamentary Debates* (1855), CXXXVII: 731-748

[8] – letter by Henry Fitz Maxse to *The Times* newspaper published 28th July 1868.

[9] – A W Kinglake Vol V pg 261.

[10] – *op cit* Walker's letter written 30th Oct 1854.

[11] – quoted in *Charge! Hurrah! Hurrah! Life of Cardigan of Balaclava* by Donald Serrell Thomas (1974) pg 242.

[12] – letters placed in the Queen's Royal Lancers Museum, Perlethorpe, Nottinghamshire.

[13] – J W Wightman *'one of the six hundred'* on the Balaclava Charge: the personal tale of a private soldier involved in this event and his subsequent time as a Russian prisoner of war (*Nineteenth Century magazine*, no.183, May 1892).

INDEX

French Zouaves, 113

G

G A Wetherall, 110
General Airey, 83, 109, 131
General Bosquet, 77, 96, 117, 118
General Campbell, 87
General Codrington, 86, 98, 120
General d'Allonville, 128, 131
General De Lacy Evans, 86
General Elie Frédéric Forey, 123
General George Buller, 103
General Henry William Adams, 99
General James Simpson, 132
General Larchey, 82
General Liprandi, 78, 89
General Marie Esme Patrice Maurice de MacMahon, 89
General Marmora, 84
General Mikhail Dmitrievich Gortschakoff, 93
General Moller, 93
General Morris, 128, 131
General Pauloff, 93, 98, 100
General Pavlov, 93
General Pennefather, 86, 100, 101, 105, 106, 108, 111, 116
General Peter Dannenberg, 93
General Pierre Bosquet, 116
General Richard Airey, 109, 127, 137, 138
General Sir Harry David Jones, 132
General Soimonoff, 93, 98, 100, 103
General Thomas Fox Strangeways, 110, 114
General Timofajeff, 93
General Todleben, 79
General Viscount Armand-Octave-Marie d'Allonville, 94
General Zhaboritski, 92
George Bullers, 90
George Cathcart, 137
George Mansell, 80
George Smith, 81
Goodlake, 87, 88, 98, 105
Graves, 88
Great Redan, 87, 89
Grenadier Guards, 91, 101, 108, 111
Gribbe, 92, 93

H

Harry Jones, 87, 88
Heavy Brigade, 78, 81, 84, 123, 91, 93, 95, 96, 97, 98, 99, 100, 101, 102, 104, 105
Henry Bentinck, 91, 101
Henry John Temple, 131
Henry Pelham Fiennes Pelham-Clinton, 89
Highland Brigade, 89, 91

Hill Bend, 107, 111
Holy Church of St Vladimir, 123
Home Ridge, 86, 87, 88, 90, 91, 96, 98, 99, 100, 101, 103, 104, 105, 106, 107, 108, 111, 112, 113, 114, 116, 117, 118, 119, 123
Hurdle, 91, 92

I

Inkerman Heights, 83

J

Jabrokritsky, 128
James Estcourt, 126, 131
James Mouat, 80
James Wightman, 99, 122
John Arthur Roebuck, 131
John Brown, 135
John McNeill, 132
John Miller Adye, 120
John Vahey, 135
Jut Road, 101

K

Kadikoi, 85, 91, 84, 91, 92, 93, 94, 95, 111, 139
Kalamata, 124
Kamara, 92, 93
Kamiesh, 91
Kazatch, 89, 91
Kerch, 80, 82, 83, 84, 90
Khrulev, 81
Kitspur, 101, 104, 107, 108, 109, 110, 111, 118, 119

L

La Marmora, 83
Lempriere, 81
Levutski, 92, 93
Lieutenant Acton, 117, 119
Lieutenant Astley, 117, 120
Lieutenant Calthorpe, 94, 100
Lieutenant Clifford, 103
Lieutenant George Johnson, 117
Lieutenant Gerald Graham, 87
Lieutenant Graham, 87
Lieutenant Landriani, 135
Lieutenant Martin, 116
Lieutenant Maxse, 126
Lieutenant Robert Bennett, 116
Lieutenant William Molesworth Cole Acton, 119
Light Brigade, 2, 73, 76, 77, 78, 79, 80, 81, 82, 83, 84, 85, 91, 118, 123, 130, 73, 75, 77, 91, 93, 96, 98, 99, 100, 101, 102, 104, 105, 122